Amazing MINI

by Peter Filby

ISBN 0 85614 060 0
A FOULIS Motoring Book
First published, by Gentry Books Ltd, 1981
Reprinted 1984,1985
© Peter Filby 1981, 84

Published by:
Haynes Publishing Group
Sparkford, Near Yeovil,
Somerset BA22 7JJ

Distributed in USA by:
Haynes Publications Inc.
861 Lawrence Drive, Newbury Park,
California 91320 USA

Dedication

To my publishers, whose patience is legendary.

Contents

Acknowledgments

Amongst the many people who have helped and encouraged me in this project I would like to express particular thanks to British Leyland and in particular Ian Elliott. I would also like to give a special thanks to the following:

National Motor Museum at Beaulieu
Cars and Car Conversions Magazine
Motor
Hot Car
Street Machine
Dave Orchard and The Mini Se7en Club
Wood & Pickett
Crayford Auto Development
Jack Daniels, Rob Golding and Graham Arnold.

A special thanks also to photographers: John Brandwood, Brian Glassborow, Mike Key, Nicky Wright and Colin Lourie.

1
Fundamental Mini

Early in August 1959 the men and women of the British motoring press were summoned to the British Motor Corporation's works at Cowley for the presentation of a new Austin/Morris model. It would be an understatement to say that they were surprised by what they saw. On the 18th and 19th of the month, members of the motoring press from all over the world were shown the same new car at the Fighting Vehicle Research and Development Establishment at Chobham, Surrey. They were startled. On the 26th of the month came the public launch, and on the day after came the reactions – the family motorist was disbelieving; the sporting motorist was completely sceptical, the hardened car buff simply thought it was all too amusing for words.

The Mini was that sort of car. It ignored so many long established design principles that it just had to create a sensation. Indeed, several of BMC's rival car manufacturers reacted rather more strongly and confidently predicted disaster. How wrong they were. But how could anybody have guessed what a remarkable impact on the world the Mini would have? How could anyone have predicted that it would set a design trend most major car manufacturers would eventually follow? How could anyone have imagined how many derivatives and offspring it would spawn? And who would have dared suggest that a mere car would become almost a pet to hundreds of thousands of owners, let alone that its name would lodge itself permanently in the English language?

When their son Alec was born in 1906 in what was then the Greek city of Smyrna, Mr and Mrs Issigonis hoped, no doubt, that he would simply do well in life. They little imagined that he would be a brilliant engineer – a genius in fact. Following the 1922 war between Turkey and Greece, the young Issigonis and his widowed mother came to Britain, where Alec began his career in engineering by studying the subject at Battersea Polytechnic and then finding a job with a small engineering firm who were trying to develop an early automatic gearbox.

A spell working for the Rootes group in the mid-1930s led Issigonis to Leonard Lord's Morris Motors in 1936, and during this pre-war period he collaborated with his friend, George Dowson, to build the famous 'Lightweight

Special', a competition machine which demonstrated the potential of all-independent suspension with rubber springs. Then, in 1948, came his first full production design, the Morris Minor, a car which so deftly took advantage of Issigonis' efficient engineering approach that it went on to become the first British car to pass the million mark. Although he spent 1952–56 working for Alvis on a 3½-litre sports saloon with rubber suspension, mid-1956 found him back with Leonard Lord and working at Longbridge for what had now become the British Motor Corporation. Within a short while Issigonis was to face his greatest challenge.

Given the type number XC9001, Issigonis' first project at Longbridge was a rear-wheel-drive 1500cc saloon which looked like a large four-door Mini and was eventually to become the front-drive BMC 1800 model. Chief assistants on this work were Jack Daniels from Morris and Chris Kingham from Alvis, both of whom were sympathetic to Issigonis' concepts and understanding of his uncompromising approach to engineering – 'making the most of the least' would describe it best. In view of the forthcoming Suez crisis, it was fortunate that these men were so united in their thinking. The talents and creative ability of this close knit team, plus those of several other key men, were to be tested to the full. It was Colonel Nasser's sudden move to nationalise and block the Suez canal in September 1956 that led to one of the most revolutionary and brilliantly designed cars in automotive history.

At a time when car makers throughout the world were celebrating the end of the post war era of austerity with larger and more lavish cars, the Suez crisis was shattering. With all UK-bound oil having to make the long, slow trek around the Cape of Good Hope, petrol rationing returned to Britain with a bang. Worse still, particularly for motoring purists like Leonard Lord, was one of the major side effects of the shortage – a sudden flood of cheap and nasty bubble cars. They had to be eradicated, preferably by a small, economical four-seater of excellent performance and BMC manufacture!

Early in 1957 Lord took the decision not to go ahead with project XC9001 or indeed with a smaller version which had also been on the cards and was type numbered XC9002 – this car later became the BMC 1100 model. What was truly needed was something even smaller yet still offering comfort for four people. And it was needed quickly.

Issigonis, Daniels and Kingham, plus their small team of draughtsmen and assistants set to work with a vengeance in March 1957. Within only four months there existed wooden mock-ups of the new car and its major components, and perhaps even more remarkable, by October there were two complete prototypes – they were nicknamed 'Orange Boxes' – undergoing their first road tests. With development continuing at such a fast pace – literally, for the 948cc A-series engines fitted to the 'Orange Boxes' were soon deemed too powerful for this type of car – it was still only July 1958 when

10

Leonard Lord sampled an 'Orange Box' for himself around the Longbridge site. He drove it, took a deep breath, and asked Issigonis to have the car in production within twelve months.

Perhaps the most remarkable aspect of this part of the Mini story is not so much the speed with which the car was created as the technical innovation with which it bristled. The transverse engine position made new demands on steering and transmission design; little was known about gearboxes mounted underneath engines and using the same sump oil; independent rubber cone suspension had not been tried on a mass production car before; there had never been ten inch diameter wheels on a 70 mph car. Indeed, when common sense indicated that the risks of putting such a design into mass production were enormous, Lord's faith in the project and in the designer seems all the more courageous. But by August 1959 everything was set for a motoring revolution.

Production was already rolling smoothly by the time the first Minis were sold late that month. Assembly lines had been installed at both the Austin works at Longbridge and the Morris works at Cowley, and at this time only the Morris version made mention of the word Mini. As it was thought important to retain the identities of the two different marques, the cars were known as the Morris Mini Minor and Austin Seven. Only much later did the word Mini come into general use for the cars, and it was even later still when the Mini officially became a marque in its own right.

BMC's initial advertising concentrated on their sensational new car's low basic price of £496 including tax. Although there were cheaper cars around, like the Ford Popular, they were very basic and old-fashioned, and it was felt that the Mini's combination of technical innovation and low cost would ensure its success. The odd thing was that despite excellent reviews in the press, the great British public did not respond particularly warmly to this somewhat startling small object designed for their transportation. The wealthy considered it too cheap and the working man perhaps thought it too clever. Even though the car had superb handling and roadholding, good performance and an incredible amount of usable space within its small dimensions, the customers were suspicious!

It was the trendy young men and women about London who started the Issigonis masterpiece on the road to success. By taking a delight both in having an easy 'parker' and a car that was classless, VIPs, trendies, film stars and famous personalities were the people who made the Mini acceptable. Once they had broken the barrier the Mini became the car for everyone–you could draw up to the Hilton in it, use it as a handy shopping basket or have fun on country roads. As for the personalities who encouraged the Mini's establishment, Lord Snowdon bought one, Laurence Harvey bought one, John Lennon drove a very special one, Peter Sellers made sure everyone got to

11

hear about his, Hayley Mills bought one and even the Queen gave it the royal seal of approval by taking a brief ride with Issigonis in Windsor Park. The Mini era was under way.

Afforded great affection by playboys and parsons, racing drivers and family men, disc jockeys and district nurses, the Mini was to become an essential ingredient of both the 'swinging sixties' and the sombre seventies. Also it was to become the perfect base for all sorts of derivatives and 'specials' built both by the BMC factory and a multitude of smaller concerns. It was to develop into a highly successful racing car both on the tracks and in rallies, and on virtually any other type of surface you would care to name! It was to be turned from a basic transport capsule into a luxury mini-Rolls Royce, both by big companies and individual customisers. Last but not least, it was to become an object of fun and great pleasure for all those who took delight in gimmicks, publicity stunts and sheer silliness. There would never be any shortage of adapatation for the Mini.

It is not the idea of this book to catalogue the development of the Mini detail by detail, but it is worth looking at some of the major stages in its life. Initially, the Austin Seven and Morris Mini Minor were each offered in two forms, basic and de-luxe, with just one engine size, 848 cc. The versatility of the basic concept began to be exploited with the estate and van versions of 1960; however development of the standard saloon saw lots of minor improvements made before the advent in September 1964 of water-filled, interconnected Hydrolastic suspension. Its job was to improve the Mini's ride quality, and though it was expensive to get into production, it proved very effective and trouble-free in service.

October 1967 brought the first major update for the Mini's styling. Changes for the Mk 2 models included a larger front grille, wider rear window, larger tail lamps and trim improvements. That same month also saw the advent of the first 1000 cc engined saloon. Few had mourned the passing of the strange floor-mounted starter button several years before, but in October 1968 many questioned the loss of the Mini's huge door pockets–the space was needed for the new wind-up window mechanisms. However, the disappearance of the exterior door hinges made the bodyshell look a bit cleaner, a detail that was attended to despite the behind-the-scenes development of a radically updated Mini.

Of course, secret restyling exercises had been tried by the Longbridge engineers several times before now, but the Mini Clubman of October 1969 was the first one that actually made it. The idea behind the extended, squared-off nose was to give the car a more modern, up-market appeal and thus help raise its price. However the job could never be called a real success, either aesthetically or practically–the Clubman's increased drag raised fuel consumption. From a cost point of view, Hydrolastic suspension had never been a success either, and by the time the Clubman appeared all Mini models were progressively returning to dry cone suspension.

The saddest part of the Mini story in the 1970s was the discontinuation of the great Mini-Cooper 1275'S' in mid-1971, thus allowing the Clubman-style 1275GT to dominate the market for nippy Minis. The rest of that decade produced a pattern of regular detail changes, all of which improved the Mini and kept it up to date without spoiling its essential character. At the time of writing, the model range consists of the basic Mini City, the 850 SDL, the 1000 SDL, the Clubman, the 1275GT and the limited edition 1100 Special. Production figures passed the one million mark in 1965, two million in 1969, three million in 1972 and four million in 1976. The total today is almost a stupendous five million!

Minis are produced at the rate of 2,500 per week and are still amongst Britain's ten best selling cars. The Mini's increasing popularity over the last 21 years is even more impressive when one considers the technological advances and rapid changes apparent in everyday life. Perhaps now that the long-awaited super-mini, the Mini Metro, has established itself so success-fully, the standard Mini will never again be Britain's third best-seller as it was in 1979, but it can at least take pride in still being around! Nowadays Sir Alec Issigonis–he was knighted in 1969–must be rather surprised that his brain-child is still around. He could never have dreamed that his hastily conceived crisis-beater would still, 21 years after its launch, be selling as well as ever. And with fuel prices always threatening to soar, it could be around for several years yet.

The secret of the Mini's success must surely be its perfectly balanced combination of perky charm and down-to-earth efficiency. Being one man's uncompromising package, it was so 'right' first time that it has been immune to passing whims and fancies. At one time the end seemed to be signalled by the Metro, but it was to the Mini's terrific credit that it even proved immune to that one. As the Austin/Morris division of today's BL Cars says, 'We know that we can never replace the Mini'.

Shown on the Cockfosters Rally in 1945, this cigar shaped racing machine was built by Alec Issigonis and his friend George Dowson for use in sprints and hillclimbs. On the face of it, the Lightweight Special has little to do with the

Mini, but under its surface the car embraced a design philosophy that Issigonis was to revive for his most famous work. This meant a stiff structure, low weight, inbuilt understeer and rubber-sprung all-independent suspension.

Built at Longbridge in 1956, project XC9001 was an important part of Issigonis' technical development towards the Mini. Although its 1500 cc ohc all-aluminium engine drove the rear wheels, the car used the Hydrolastic interconnected suspension system and featured a particularly space-efficient interior. It also showed what an early four-door Mini could have looked like.

Early in 1957, BMC supremo Sir Leonard Lord gave the go-ahead for a new small car which he wanted in production as soon as possible. Thanks to the Suez crisis, petrol rationing had hit Britain and brought with it a panic reaction that transformed the sales charts of bubble car manufacturers almost overnight! Lord was horrified, hence this wooden mock-up of what was then called project XC9003 which was completed in only four months.

Nicknamed 'Orange Box' because of its colour, this is one of two pre-production prototype Minis which were put on the road in October 1957, only eight months after the first designs had been drawn on paper. Disguised with Austin A35 radiator grilles, the cars were tested almost entirely at night.

In this photograph XC9003 has been developed further, and with the exception of its radiator grille and indicators, differs little from the production Mini. Designed to seat four people in full comfort and hopefully sweep the plague of bubble cars from British roads, XC9003 was the start of a project that was to break many established rules and eventually become a legend.

The 'Orange Boxes' differed from their future production sisters in several ways; obvious changes were their use of sheet metal structures rather than subframes and their engine installations the opposite way round to the eventual set-up. But the sheet metal structures proved too prone to metal fatigue and the engines were turned round to stop the carburettors icing-up and give the inlet valves more shelter.

Opposite: With Sir Leonard Lord saying, 'You can use any sort of engine you like as long as we have it on our present production lines', Alec Issigonis made the obvious choice – the Austin A35/Morris Minor A-Series unit. This particular version shown is the 948 cc which was used only in the 'Orange Boxes' as it was considered too powerful for the type of customers the first Minis were to be aimed at. Indeed, the story goes that BMC's testers used to have a whale of a time in their 'Orange Boxes' racing the Jaguars that shared their road test route to Cirencester and back.

Amazing Mini

Driven by Jack Daniels, who was number two to Issigonis on what was now officially termed the ADO15 project (ADO stood for Austin Drawing Office), this is production prototype Mini number five undergoing water tests at Coughton Ford. These tests did not solve the problem of water leaks on early Minis and the obvious joke was that every customer was given a free pair of Wellington boots to protect him from the rotting carpets!

After an incredibly short development period by normal mass production car standards, BMC's bubble-car burster was publicly launched on the 26th August 1959, being offered for sale simultaneously in nearly 100 countries. The basic version was priced at only £496 including tax while the de-luxe version, as shown here, cost £537.

Although the word 'Mini' was eventually to become an established term in the English language, being used for anything from holidays to computers, it was not at first intended for general use with ADO15. While the Morris version's name was linked to Issigonis's previous success, the Morris Minor, by being called the Mini Minor, the Austin version was initially known as the Austin Seven. This shot shows an early production Seven posing with an original Seven, a 1929 coachbuilt saloon.

The secret of the Mini's success was that it was considerably smaller than its competitors; it offered more space inside and retained excellent performance. In this shot of a special cutaway car, you can clearly see the wicker basket that was designed to fit under the rear seat and take the space utilisation theme even further.

In those wonderful carefree days before yellow lines, parking meters and authoritative meter matrons, the Mini's ability to park in a tight space was perhaps more important than it is today. At ten foot from end to end, the car could easily be slotted into a gap only 18 inches longer.

Opposite: *The blurb on BMC's early advertisements was absolutely unquestionable. Seating four adults in comfort, endowed with superb roadholding and controllability, capable of 70 mph and giving up to 50 mpg, the Mini was indeed a revolution.*

IT'S WIZARDRY
ON WHEELS
THE
Revolutionary
"QUALITY FIRST"
MORRIS
Mini-Minor

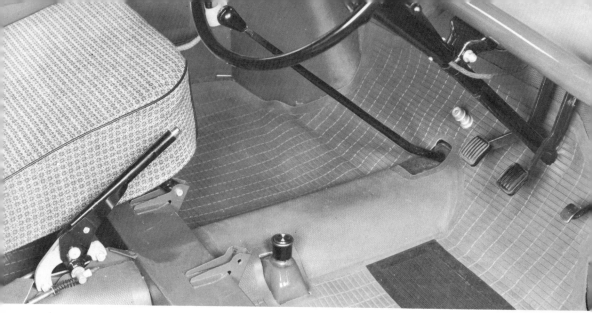

Early prototypes had a seat trim style which never got into production. However, the straight gear lever was used for a short time and the strange floor-mounted, press-button starter lasted a whole two years.

Opposite: *In this shot of the Longbridge factory, Mini body shells on the overhead conveyor are ready to be mated with their subframe and power train assemblies. Normal production for a day shift on the assembly line was 24 cars an hour, each worker having a maximum of close on two and a half minutes to finish his particular job. Thus with 57 different stations for each car, total construction time per unit was just over two hours.*

To add to the basic and de-luxe models, a new 'Super' saloon Mini was introduced in September 1961. Apart from minor trim changes, extra noise insulation and a two-tone paint scheme, it also heralded the introduction of a key start ignition switch and oil pressure plus water temperature gauges. Note also the revised gear lever.

People still love 'em: This is not an early publicity shot but a photograph taken in 1980. Owned by Mini enthusiast Linda Sturgess, the car is a November 1959 example with only 32,000 miles on the clock. In absolutely immaculate condition with not a spot of rust, it is used only for special events and must be something of a collector's item.

Opposite: *Although the quilted sound-deadening material behind the engine in this photograph was peculiar to early versions of the Super de-luxe Mini introduced in October 1962, the model's engine installation was typical of any 850 Mini.*

Linda Sturgess' car has an original interior. It was the use of sliding windows that allowed room for those marvellous door pockets that seemed to hold everything bar the kitchen sink. They were much mourned when the advent of wind-up windows forced them out of business in 1968.

Although Minis were exported to many parts of the world, this particular car is more than just an export model. Distinguished by its lack of external seams and the lip running round the wheel arches and sills, it is one of the glassfibre bodied cars made in the experimental shops at Longbridge to help establish an assembly operation in Chile–where there was no machinery for pressing steel.

Mini car with mini skirt–a predictable enough comment, perhaps, but a very relevant one just the same. After a slow sales start, the Mini had eventually caught on in a big way thanks to the many 'trendies' around the big cities who found it the ideal fast runabout. This car is a Mk 2 model, as introduced in 1967 and distinguished by a larger front grille, a wider rear window and new rear lights.

Mini fever was running strong by the mid-sixties, so when the car's tenth anniversary came up in 1969, it was an ideal opportunity for enthusiasts to show their appreciation of a remarkable little car.

In October 1968 the standard 850 Mini had at last been relieved of its ugly exterior door hinges and given wind-up windows plus dry cone suspension. Prior to this, in 1967, the Mini 1000 had been introduced with 998 cc power and a remote gear-shift, so when the first Mini Clubman appeared in October 1969 it naturally combined the best of both sister models and added a restyled front end for good measure. Where it lost out, though, was on typical Mini 'appeal' and styling balance.

Still spartan, but much better equipped than the first Mini interiors, this layout belongs to an early Clubman. Note the stalk controls and fresh air vents.

Minis were crash tested into concrete blocks right from the early days, but this one is a Clubman meeting the 30 mph crash safety requirements at the Mira road research laboratory.

Introduced in October 1969 alongside the Clubman, the Mini 1275GT offered better braking and higher performance from its single carburettor engine – so much so that it was deemed fit to replace the standard 998 cc Mini Cooper.

By now Sir Alec, this picture was taken at the great man's retirement party in 1971. With other landmarks of his career in the background, he poses with the very first Mini built. The production total of the day speaks for itself.

Opposite: Another Mini 1275GT, this time in component form showing the various major panels and components which make up the car.

Aiming for more positive gear selection, this rod shift assembly was introduced on all Mini models early in 1973.

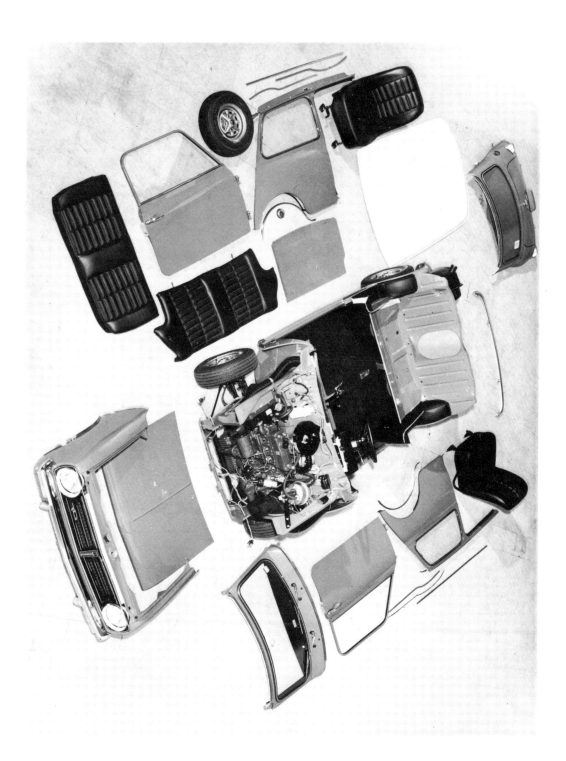

This car is a Canadian specification export model. The side repeater lamps and ugly raised bumpers were, like the more powerful heater and extra exhaust emission equipment, a result of having to meet regulations across the water.

It's 1976 and four million Minis have been built in a remarkable production run which nobody could have predicted back in 1959. The trouble was that by this time mini-skirts had long since gone out of favour, meaning that an obliging Miss Great Britain, Sue Cuff, agreed to cut her dress short specially for the occasion. Needless to say, she was a Mini fan.

In August 1977, Dunlop Denovo wheels and tyres, tinted glass, reversing lamps and a locking fuel filler cap all became standard equipment on the 1275GT. But the car's blunt front compares very badly with the lines of 16 year old model Joanna Latham, for whom this assignment started a career which led to a Playboy centre spread in 1979.

Compared with the original Mini's price of £496, the £2,288 'budget' Mini City was still good value when introduced in August 1979. It featured trendy black and white houndstooth check cloth seat centre panels, in place of the previous all-PVC trim, black bumpers and individual side stripes.

At the same time as introducing the Mini City, BL also turned to the other end of the scale by introducing a Super-de-luxe version of the Mini 850 with fabric seating, additional gauges, face level vents, map pockets and opening rear windows. And here you see it like you have never seen it before–this publicity shot was deemed out of character for the Mini market and thus you are now being treated to a first public viewing!

To celebrate 20 marvellous years of Mini production, the £3,300 Mini 1100 Special was launched in August 1979. To commemorate the birthday of Britain's most successful car design, this model was the most lavishly equipped production Mini ever and was limited to a production run of only 5,000. External features were an exclusive colour scheme with side striping, a vinyl roof and wide alloy wheels covered by black wheel arch extensions.

What a difference from the original Mini interior! The 1100 Special owner was treated to special woven seat centre panels, a soft-grip steering wheel, 1275GT-style dash with padded top rail, passenger's oddment box below the parcel shelf, oddment tray around the gear lever and a neatly integrated centre console housing a push-button radio, a quartz clock and a cigar lighter.

The major celebration for the Mini's 20th birthday was the Mini Extravaganza held at Donington Park race circuit in August 1979. The day included displays,

competitions for various categories of Minis and this special parade around the track.

Following a TV commercial which a patriotic Spike Milligan performed free to help the cause, secretary Sue Cooke from South Wales bought this Union Jack Mini to do her bit of flag waving. It was almost twenty years after the introduction date, and still the Mini was encouraging the sort of affection normally reserved for rather more elegant and desirable motor cars.

40

2
Maximum Mini

Right from the very beginnings of the Mini project, Alec Issigonis and BMC's development engineers realised that they were going to be able to squeeze maximum mileage from the one basic concept. However, they could hardly have guessed what other serious car builders and extrovert characters would get up to over the years, but they could certainly see how far the 'official' line could be followed.

What made it all so easy was the front engine/front drive layout which allowed complete freedom of design from the pedals backwards. Having all the suspension, as well as the engine and gearbox, on separate subframes meant that they could simply be attached to any body/chassis unit for almost any purpose.

The first of what were to be many BMC-developed Mini variants was launched early in 1960. It was the Mini van, a spartan vehicle which gave little indication of the much more exciting variants to come, but which was still unexpectedly important in its own right. Indeed, the van contributed very heavily towards total Mini output over the first two years of production, and helped a great deal towards propping up the poor early sales figures of the saloons. The reason for this was that the Government had exempted vans from purchase tax on the grounds that they were business vehicles, and thus for a mere £360 people could take advantage of all the technical innovation for which they would otherwise have to pay £496 if buying the saloon! Business use or not, it did not take many private owners long to realise what a bargain they were getting.

Of course, apart from being a poor man's sports car, the Mini van also did a very good job of being a working van, and had an interior capacity of 46 cubic feet plus an additional 12 cubic feet if one bothered to remove the passenger seat; and for a van it was no slouch, even though it used the standard 848 cc engine. For those who wanted a similar load carrying capacity but with less utility, the first Mini Countryman/Traveller estate cars were introduced in September 1960 with stuck-on timbers (which later became optional) to create a traditional rustic look. Like the vans, these variants had a longer wheelbase than the saloon whilst retaining the standard engine. Along with the rest of the Mini model range, the estates gained Mk. 2 status in 1967, being fitted at the same time with the 998 cc engine – this unit was only offered as an option for the van at the time, although it did become standard later on.

Early in 1961 came the ultimate Mini utility – the pick-up, again with 848 cc power. As the vans were already proving, particularly with the AA, RAC and Post Office, these variants made excellent and reliable delivery wagons, and the pick-up was soon at home on farms and building sites. But while van, pick-up and estate Minis are all still in production today, the latter has been offered only in Clubman form since 1969 – the same cannot unfortunately be said for BMC's early attempts at up-market Minis.

The Riley Elf and Wolseley Hornet were both launched in October 1961 – to the delight of the marketing men and the groans of the engineers, Issigonis included. Mechanically identical to the basic Mini, the cars were distinguished by traditional-style grilles, separate sidelight indicator units, completely re-vised rear bodywork with proper boots, and uprated interiors with walnut veneered dashboards and key-activated ignition. They certainly represented the start of a specialist trend for Mini limousines, but where they suffered was in retaining 848 cc power to shift all that extra weight. Thus in November 1962 both cars were given Mk. 2 designation plus single carburettor 998 cc engines. They also went through changes with Hydrolastic suspension, wind-up windows, concealed door hinges and so on, but suffered early extermination in 1969 following the merger between BMH (BMC plus Jaguar) and the Leyland Motor Corporation. Total production figures for the Elf and Hornet respectively were 30,912 and 28,455.

In marked contrast to BMC's two specialist luxury Minis was a Mini variant of a totally different nature which was launched at the same time in October 1961. Already the standard Mini had got itself a reputation for being something of a sports car with the more sprightly members of the public, who had quickly learnt how to extract maximum fun from its fine blend of performance and roadholding. Quite naturally this had instantly created a demand for even more performance, and the Mini was soon putting a broad smile on the faces of owners of tuning concerns. Although the Cooper operation at Surbiton had previously concentrated on the construction of highly successful Grand Prix cars, John Cooper's friendship with Alec Issigonis soon led to his use of an early Mini for everyday transport. And therein lay the seed of a legend.

John Cooper's thinking was that BMC would gain a great deal of prestige by producing a more rapid Mini with a tuned Cooper-modified engine, front disc brakes, a remote gear lever and improved trim. The car would be designed not so much for competition as for the everyday use of competition drivers and those who simply wanted to get a move on in life. Issigonis was not entirely happy about the idea, but Cooper eventually obtained BMC's

42

agreement to a trial production run of 1,000 cars. The car was to be known as the Mini Cooper and a new engine was to be developed using all the experience Cooper had gained with his Formula Junior version of the A-series engine.

The first Mini Cooper was finally announced in October 1961 at a price of £679; producing 55 bhp, its twin-carb 997 cc engine could push the little box to 60 mph in 17.2 seconds and it achieved a maximum speed of 85.2 mph. Both of these figures were substantially better than those of the standard Mini. Even Issigonis became enthusiastic!

The rest of the Mini Cooper story is, of course, well known. Despite the original intentions, right from the start the car totally transformed the Mini's reputation in the competition world. In 1962 alone it grabbed 153 successes in varied motoring events all over the world. Accordingly, the private tuners now got down to making the car even faster. When Daniel Richmond, owner of Downton Engineering, produced an example which was as fast in third gear as the standard Mini Cooper when it was flat out in top, the Longbridge men took great notice. Their answer was the fiery Mini Cooper 'S' of March 1963.

The first engine to be used in the 'S' was the short stroke 1071 cc unit producing 70 bhp at 6200 rpm, and amongst many enthusiasts this one was to become the favourite of all Cooper engines. Next, early in 1964, came the 1275 cc and 970 cc 'S' units, the 1071 being discontinued later that same year. Early in 1965 the 970 engine was also dropped, and this left the 1275 car to continue a pattern of steady development through Mk. 2 and Mk. 3 versions until one sad day in June 1971 when Longbridge said goodbye to the last in the line. A great name had died, but with the collector/classic car movement already under way a large number of the total of 145,493 Minis, Cooper and Cooper 'S' were assured of immortality.

The last works–built Mini derivative covered by this chapter is the Mini Moke, a very different kettle of fish from the Mini Cooper but, just the same, one which created incredible affection among its followers. It started life early in the 1960's as a basic personnel wagon which was sent to the Fighting Vehicle Research and Development Establishment at Chobham for serious testing under the scrutiny of several armies. Hitched to the very basic, 80 inch wheelbase, all-steel body/chassis unit were standard Mini subframes and running gear, power being from the 848 cc engine. Being lightweight and easy to handle, the Moke was expected to have several useful military applications but in the end let itself down through poor ground clearance. So, it was offered to the general public – some of them loved it and some of them hated it!

The first time customers could buy a Moke was in August 1964. As already indicated, you had to be something of an extrovert – and definitely a masochist – to be happy with the spartan motorised platform in Britain's inclement weather; but on a warm sunny day it was the ultimate in motoring freedom and a sheer delight. The trouble, of course, was that there were never enough warm, sunny days on home territory and thus the Moke met with very poor sales. However, the export story was rather better, the car being used in many warm climates as an open-air fun taxi or handy light truck. This, together with the Customs and Excise department's refusal to keep it in their commercial vehicle category and thus free of Purchase Tax, led it quite logically to production in Australia. With the last British-made Mokes leaving the lines in October 1968, the total constructed reached 14,518 of which no less than 89.9% had been exported. Down under, the Moke simply went from strength to strength, and the irony of this was that examples were soon being despatched all the way back to Britain and Europe; this interest even now provides one specialist London company with healthy and regular sales.

Though the Moke is now firmly ensconsed in Australia, its continued success shows how well its straightforward Mini basis has stood the test of time. The Riley Elf, Wolseley Hornet, Mini Cooper and Cooper 'S' have all gone too – to the great car scrapyard in the sky – but both the Mini van and pick-up are still demonstrating capably the versatility of the original layout. It is highly unlikely that there will ever be any more factory-built Mini derivatives, but the Issigonis concept lives on in the Mini Metro and who knows how many varieties that car will bring?

Utility Mini. The big advantage of Alec Issigonis' Mini was that its front engine, front-wheel-drive layout allowed complete freedom of design from the front bulkhead backwards. Offered for sale in May 1960, the Mini van was the first of a whole series of BMC-built Mini variants.

With a longer wheelbase than the saloon and an overall length increased by ten inches, the Mini van had an interior capacity of 46 cubic feet, more if the passenger seat was removed. Along with other large organisations like the AA and RAC, the Post Office found the van ideal as a daily workhorse and ordered thousands of them.

Piggy Mini. The Traveller or Countryman estate car was put on the market in September 1960. The design was an ideal compromise between the contrasting themes of carrying capacity and saloon-style comfort, the Countryman's stick-on timbers giving it the traditional rustic look that the landed gentry were known to prefer.

More pigs! This time the unfortunate animals are helping to demonstrate the usefulness of the Mini pick-up, as introduced in January 1961. Like the van

and estate, it used the standard 848 cc engine.

The original twin-carb 997cc engine with remote gearchange. Pushing out 55bhp, it could accelerate the little Mini Cooper to 60mph in 17.2 seconds

(*compared with 27.1 seconds for the standard Mini*) *and to a top speed of 85 mph.
Its effect in the competition world was to be enormous.*

Little did Grand Prix racing car manufacturer and tuning wizard John Cooper realise what he was starting when he acquired a production Mini and proceeded to warm it up somewhat. Introduced in October 1961 at a total price of £679 7s 3d, the 997cc Mini Cooper Mk.1 was originally conceived as a limited production road car for those who wanted to get a move on in life. A weekly output of only 25 cars was on the cards right at the start! Disc brakes were standard.

Mini with dignity. With its upright radiator following the traditional marque shape, the Riley Elf was announced in October 1961 to combine an up-market image with the Mini's established virtues. The Wolseley Hornet was introduced alongside the Elf and featured a very similar frontal treatment.

Following the advent of the 997 cc Cooper, Minis had little option but to get faster and be even more fun! The terrific 1071 cc Cooper 'S' of 1963 and the 998 cc 'ordinary' Cooper of early 1964 quickly led to the long-stroked 1275 cc Cooper 'S', an example of which is depicted here attempting a head-over-heels. There was also a 970 'S', which only served to confuse matters and was dropped in 1965 soon after the 1071 car had met a similar fate.

Left: *For the first year of their lives, the Elf and Hornet used the standard 848 cc Mini engine. In view of the car's extra weight, it was not surprising that their performance suffered, and a year after their introduction they were fitted with a single carburettor version of what was in 1964 to become the 998 cc Cooper engine.*

55

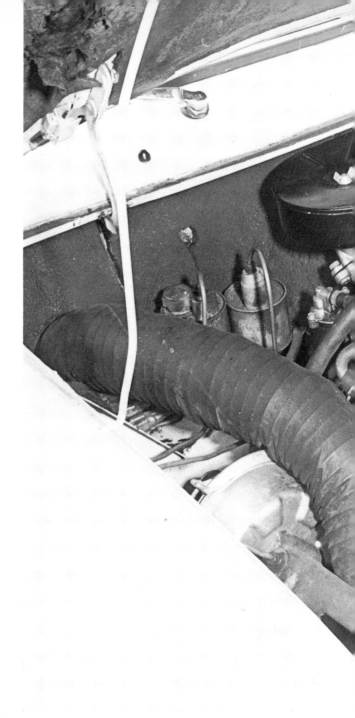

The 1275 cc Cooper 'S' engine produced 76 bhp at 5900 rpm and enabled the Mini's high standards of handling and roadholding to be exploited to the full. What a shame John Cooper never got the chance to try his ideas for an 1800 'S' unit!

A Wolseley Hornet displays the lengthened tail it shared with the Riley Elf and which increased boot capacity from the standard Mini's 5.5 cubic feet to 8 cubic feet. The two models also shared wood veneered facias and two-tone paint schemes.

Opposite: BMC continued to exploit the tremendous versatility of the Mini concept by coming up with this spartan light personnel carrier in the early sixties. The idea was that it could readily be lifted by a helicopter, could carry four men fairly quickly and could even be man-handled out if it became stuck in soft ground. Called the Moke, the 848 cc powered machine was seriously evaluated by several armies before being pronounced impractical and reduced to a different role as a simple fun car.

58

The Moke was finally made available to the public in August 1964–in a somewhat revised form from its earlier military design. Although there was no shortage of trendies, extroverts and masochists happy to drive the spartan utility vehicle

in British weather, the Moke was much more at home in situations like this – on the beach in the south of France.

In 1968, Moke production in Britain was discontinued in favour of a move to Australia. In a more suitable climate the spartan motorised platform became very popular and soon different versions, like this pick-up, were appearing.

Musical Minis. The Moke had a multitude of applications, one of the best being an open-air taxi in warm climates like the West Indies. Here a batch of cars are shown doing a similar job for the Terry Lightfoot jazzmen at the less exotic venue of Brands Hatch. The occasion was a Mini Festival in 1967.

Well before the standard and Cooper 'S' Minis received their wind-up windows during the period 1968–70, the up-market Wolseley Hornet and Riley Elf received theirs in 1966. This interior belongs to an Elf Mk. 3.

The Wolseley Hornet interior was much less refined than the Elf's, with the polished wood looking completely out of place on the little oval dashboard.

The Mk. 3 Wolseley Hornet, as introduced in October 1966, was distinguished by its concealed door hinges and higher standard of interior fittings. Along with the Elf, the Hornet was discontinued in August 1969, the total production number of both models resting at 59,367.

It's 1967, and the Mini Cooper 1275 'S' has been revised into Mk. 2 form with external changes like a new grille, wider rear window and new rear lights. It's a shame they did not revise the dashboard too!

Another factory-built Mini variant was the 998cc powered Clubman Estate introduced in October 1969. It replaced the original Countryman and Traveller Minis, and was really the only Mini which looked properly balanced with a Clubman front.

Almost 20 years after its introduction, the Mini van was still Britain's best-selling small van with annual sales approaching 10,000 units. Early in 1980, the 998 cc model was improved with Mini City-type trim, including special seats, extra sound deadening and nylon carpeting, the idea being to provide car-style comfort.

Opposite: Final version of the much loved Mini Cooper 'S' was the Mk. 3 introduced in March 1970. It was distinguished by its wind-up windows, concealed door hinges and Clubman-type door trim and seats. Sadly it was out of production again by July 1971, being dropped in favour of the 1275GT. The 'S' had been a great little car, and its passing was mourned by many thousands of enthusiasts.

3
Prototype Mini

While many straightforward variations on the Mini theme – for instance, the vans, estates, Hornets, Coopers and so on – were envisaged for full production right from the word 'go', there was also a remarkable number of Mini-based prototypes under development throughout the car's life. Although none of them reached the showrooms, they represented an intriguing range of vehicles, some perhaps offering opportunities which should not have been missed by BMC/BL.

Even before the Mini's introduction, BMC's engineers mocked-up the sort of car which they felt a rival manufacturer could come up with as a Mini basher. It's easy now to laugh at the odd-looking DO19, as it was designated, but in those days its maximum space concept might have been perfectly feasible for production, had not the layout offered little protection to passengers in the event of an accident. Anyway, it was only the start of a great deal of research aimed at keeping the Mini ahead of its competitors. Yet little could the engineers have guessed how capably the Issigonis master-piece was going to do that anyway.

Perhaps one serious mistake BMC made was in not manufacturing a Mini-based two-seater or 2+2 sports car. The first opportunity was ADO34, a project for which both Longbridge and Abingdon built open and closed prototypes in 1960. Although nothing sensational compared to what some of Britain's specialist manufacturers were dreaming up for the Mini, they were all fairly attractive and would have found a ready market had BMC been able to justify making them at the same time as Abingdon was making the new MG Midget and Austin Healey Sprite. However the ADO70 was much more of a missed opportunity than the ADO34.

Better known as the Michelotti Mini, ADO70 was a chunkily attractive front engined sports car, built by the Turin coachbuilders in 1970 at a time when the Midget and Sprite were beginning to look rather long in the tooth. And ADO70 was nothing if not modern, with loads of space in its cockpit, a large boot and a neat removable roof panel. Yet, with very little foresight, the powers-that-be decided that they could not justify the cost of getting the car into America and promptly cancelled the project – so leaving the way wide open for the not too dissimilar Fiat X1/9.

Other Mini-based prototypes, mocked-up or built in running form over the years, involved long ones, wide ones, ones with boots and several variations on the Moke theme, but obviously the most important thoughts running through the development engineers' minds by the late sixties centred on a possible replacement for the Mini. In 1968, Issigonis himself came up with a new car which was seriously considered for production. Called 9X, it was roughly Mini size but had more legroom, wind-up windows, a hatchback and conventional suspension – MacPherson strut at the front and trailing arms plus coil springs at the rear. It also had styling which lost the Mini's cheeky individuality, so perhaps it was just as well that 9X was dropped around the time of BMC's merger with Leyland.

Another project which was well advanced at the time of cancellation was ADO74, an altogether bigger car than the Mini which, in view of motoring's changing pattern over the last two years, might well have been a worthy addition to BL's range. But it was in 1976 that the Mini was most seriously threatened by a possible replacement. The car in question was ADO88, a modern Mini, which solved the Issigonis car's old problems of elbow room, noisiness and poor ride. However, ADO88 was not particularly elegant and gave way in 1978 to LC8, a development along the same lines but altogether much more pleasing. This was the car that became the Metro.

The fanfare of the Metro's arrival in full production can hardly have been missed by anyone in the civilised world, and its continuing success is something upon which the future survival of BL as a major car manufacturer heavily depends. But although the Metro is the one Mini-based prototype which finally made it, what is most significant is that it was decided early on that it would *not* replace the Mini. Indeed, there will probably never be any more Mini projects at Longbridge. What is the point? By all accounts, one quite amazing little car is virtually indestructible.

Around the time the Mini was being put into production, it was decided that BMC's engineers should mock-up the sort of car which other manufacturers might come up with as a competitor. Obviously the result of some very 'free' thinking, this device was known as DO19 and is pictured in the styling studio at Longbridge.

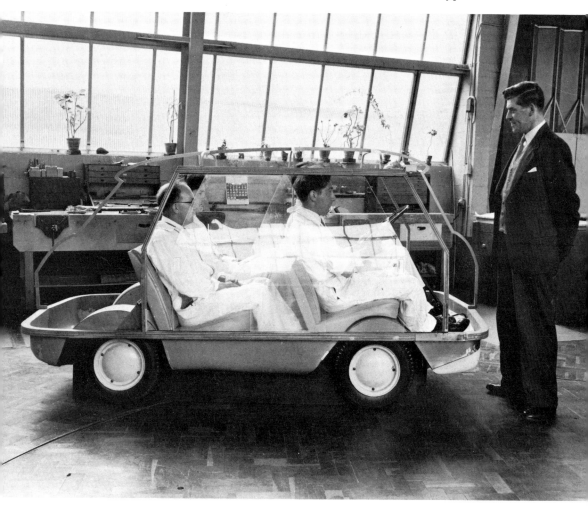

DO19 was planned to be rear-engined and take full advantage of available space. This brought the feet of the front seat occupants into what was considered a dangerous position in the event of an accident, and it was this which quickly killed off the project.

ADO34 was a project for a front-engined, Mini-based sports car which was under review soon after the Mini's 1959 launch. Several variations of the theme were tried, this one probably being one of the efforts produced at Longbridge and styled by Dick Burzi. The hardtop looks as though it was removable.

While Longbridge started the ADO34 idea, the engineers at Abingdon were also allowed to have a go at it. But the success of the Mini-Cooper and the announcement of the new Austin Healey Sprite-based MG Midget in 1961 soon put paid to any hopes of producing this chunkily attractive car.

Built to the same wheelbase as the Mini van, Abingdon's ADO34 used straight-forward Mini subframes and suspension units. It was proposed as either a convertible or with a fastback hardtop.

Another variation on the Mini-based ADO34 theme was this Austin Healey-badged mock-up built at Abingdon. Visible through the windscreen is what would have been a metal tonneau cover to go over the two small rear seats.

While BMC were displaying several Mini variants on their stand at the 1961 Motor Show, this handsome prototype could be seen on the Zagato stand. Built on a Mini van chassis, the glassfibre body had room for four adults and featured a roomy boot. Sad to say, it became yet another lost cause.

MG and Mini never did get it together. Although Wolseley and Riley Minis were produced, for some reason this proposed MG Mini never got beyond the stage of drawings.

K AS AUSTIN and MORRIS MINI

SAME BONNET AS HORN

SAME AS WOLSEL

NEW M.G. GRILLE TO FIT BONNET

Very early in 1963, Alec Issigonis completed the installation of two engines (a 950 cc unit forward and an 848 cc aft) in an unsuspecting Moke shell – in fact, one of the very first made. Called the Mighty Moke, the four-wheel-drive bad conditions-beater was prompted by the appalling weather of that winter. It is shown here ploughing through the snow on the lawn at Longbridge, with Jack Daniels driving.

Although there was a vague suggestion that the twin-engined Moke could be made available to the public, only the U.S. Army was ever allowed to get its hands on the model. About six examples were built in all.

The Twini-Moke, as it came to be known, had an experimental 1100 cc engine at each end. Each engine could be started individually and either used individually or in tandem. The main disadvantage was the lack of load carrying ability.

Opposite: *Apart from trying out a single-engined, four-wheel-drive Moke, the prototype shop at Longbridge also built this short version with a $72\frac{1}{2}$ inch wheel base. But like all the others, nothing ever came of it.*

Looking a little like a mobile packing case, this mock-up was a development of the Moke theme probably built around the mid-sixties.

The amazing Ant, a Mini-engined, four-wheel-drive workhorse born around 1967. Several of these machines were made (possibly as many as 25) and sent all over the world for evaluation. This one was used by the U.S. Army Tank Automotive Command.

The extermination of the Ant came upon the formation of British Leyland in 1968 when an example was sent to Rover. Back came the reply that the company would rather not have any competition for the Land Rover.

This mock-up of a modified Mini bodyshell was distinguished by its curved side windows. It was known as the 'barrel' Mini!

Completed in 1968, the 9X was Alec Issigonis' interpretation of a Mini replacement. It had wind-up windows, more legroom, conventional suspension and a new, more compact overhead camshaft engine. But the styling lost all the sheer individuality of the Mini, and in the end Issigonis was not concerned that 9X was dropped around the time of the merger with Leyland.

Opposite: Using many Mini parts, including subframes, suspension and steering, this chirpy looking electric car was designed by Michelotti and built jointly by British Leyland and Crompton Leyland Electricars. Purely a research exercise, it was shown at the 1972 Geneva Motor Show.

Completed in 1974, the Mini SRV4 was an experimental safety vehicle designed to survive any incident better than its standard sister. Its stretched wheelbase allowed a clear crush space behind the engine and the ugly nose structure was

designed to absorb and distribute impact loads–pedestrians for instance! Also, the door sills were strengthened and the suspension improved.

What a shame the Michelotti Mini did not become Britain's answer to the Fiat X1/9! With its attractive shape and removable roof, it could surely have done the job. However, the problem was that the American market would have been very important to the car's success and getting it over there meant large investment in order to comply with legislation; and BL didn't have the money.

Opposite top: *This neat little Mini-based sports car was code named ADO70 but was more commonly called Michelotti Mini, the Turin coachbuilders having been responsible for building it in 1970. The basis of the car was a Mini 1275GT taken from the original production batch late in 1969 and driven out to Italy for the job. Underneath the steel body, all running gear remained standard 1275GT.*

Opposite bottom: *To solve the old Mini complaint of lack of elbow room, a 1275GT was given eight inches extra width in 1973. But like so many other good ideas developed by the company's engineers over the years, it went no further.*

92

Although cancelled in March 1974, ADO74 was a serious project which could have finally killed the Mini, it was bigger than the Mini; and featured MacPherson strut suspension. It would have competed directly with the Ford Fiesta had BL been able to afford £130 million to put it into production. This is one of several styling variations which were prepared.

Designed by Harris Mann, ADO88 bore something of a family resemblance to the Metro but had a more upright rear end. It is significant that after all the projects aimed at replacing the Mini, ADO88 failed to do so and even the Metro was designed to sell alongside *the Issigonis masterpiece.*

The car which came nearest to replacing the Mini was ADO88. Developed in 1976 and heavily camouflaged in this picture, it made no radical changes to the Mini concept apart from the areas of elbow room, noise and ride. However, when Michael Edwardes took over as BL supremo, it was dropped in favour of the very similar but slightly smaller LC8, otherwise known as the Metro.

A selection of types across the years. A 1968 Cooper, 1983 City 1000 and an early Traveller or Countryman Estate. (Lindsay Porter)

An example of the new-style front end introduced in October 1969 on the Clubman model.

Above: *Mark Williams' Cooper 'S' trying very hard in a hillclimb. (Alan Jeffrey)*

Below: *A mini beautifully prepared for Mini Modsaloon racing. (Chris Harvey)*

Above: *An example of specialist coachbuilding, shown to good effect by one of Wood and Pickett's luxurious Minis. (Wood and Pickett)*

Below: *The GTM, one of the most popular and long-lived special bodied Minis. (Chris Whiteman)*

4
Competition Mini

In 1959 the Mini could hardly have been considered a fast car, let alone a competition car with great potential. Indeed, the prospect of using it as a *road* car caused much amusement in some circles, so it must have been with a certain amount of scepticism that people listened to the ambitious competition plans of those who were clever enough to spot the little box's great promise. To have faith in the sporting ability of that stubby little profile and those tiny wheels took some nerve in those days, yet those who believed in the Mini were to be justified. On the British competition scene, the car was to become just about the most popular competition machine ever: around the world it was to become legendary.

The point that the sceptics missed was that the Mini had all the right characteristics for racing. Exceptional cornering power and great stability came about thanks to the combination of front wheel drive, a low centre of gravity, independent suspension and a wheel track of only four inches less than the overall height. Although the short blunt nose was rather an aerodynamic handicap, there was certainly no shortage of power to overcome this. The tuning business already knew about the A-series engine as it had spent years developing the same basic unit in the Austin A35 and Morris Minor. The engine's reliability in highly tuned form had been perfected too, so all the basic ingredients for a successful competition career were present; and sure enough, right from the start Minis began to show what they could do.

They were not necessarily very fast and their braking performance did not inspire too much confidence, but their handling was beyond reproach and their diminutive size a great advantage. Very soon Minis were delighting drivers and spectators alike with their ability to pass at will on the outside or inside of corners–it really did not matter! The engine size of the opposition did not pose any problems, Minis being able to scuttle around much bigger cars at corners in a really delightful fashion. Within weeks of entering battle, competition Minis were winning driving tests. Within months, they were winning their class in saloon car racing. Within only a year or two, they were hovering on the verge of international rally success and outright racing victories. There were problems of course, one of the first being the way the cars began to lose wheels at a rather alarming rate. But development soon took care of their deficiencies, a whole range of competition extras becoming available from BMC's competitions department at Abingdon and other tuning shops.

In circuit racing, the Mini drivers who came to prominence early on included John Aley, Doc Shepherd, Christabel Carlisle, Bill Aston and Sir John Whitmore. In rallying, it was names like John Handley, Pat Moss (sister of Stirling), Ann Wisdom and Warwick Banks. When the Mini-Cooper arrived on the competition scene in 1962, the Mini's reputation was strengthened to an astonishing degree, no less than 153 successes being recorded that year in various events in all parts of the world. The Cooper brought along more famous names, those of Rauno Aaltonen, Timo Makinen, Paddy Hopkirk, John Fitzpatrick and – most spectacular of them all – John Rhodes.

Perhaps the Mini's greatest period in competition was the mid-1960's. Proving its true competition worth and giving a strong warning of things to come, the car, with Paddy Hopkirk at the wheel, first won the great Monte Carlo Rally in 1964. This was followed with another win, by Timo Makinen, in 1965, a disqualification from 1st place in 1966 and yet another victory in 1967. During the same period, the circuit racers were burning tyres everywhere, delighting the crowds and generally securing the Mini's standing as a legend in its own time. One would-be racing driver of that period was a fellow named James Hunt. His first ever racer was a Mini he built himself in 1966 from parts acquired from several trips round the breakers' yards. Hunt did not have any wins with the car, in fact he only raced it twice, but the point is that it started him off. Niki Lauda was another famous Formula One driver whose early years involved a Mini.

The list of drivers who have raced Minis and the list of their successes go on and on running right up to the present moment. For Minis are still to be found battling it out in various forms of competition – autocross, rallycross, hill climbing, circuit racing, sand racing, hot rod racing and other more obscure events. Maybe the days have gone when the little box could pulverise most of its opposition in big international rallies and major circuit events, but the Mini today can still provide more enthusiasts with more fun at less cost than any other car.

Oops, nearly overdid it! Despite the fact that the Mini enjoyed sensational cornering ability, this shot somehow epitomises the car in competition and was taken at Gurston Down hillclimb in the early 1960's.

Opposite: *Although they quickly proved their ability on the race circuits and in rallies, Minis found long distance trials not to their liking. This is R. W. Slone being towed up Darracott in the Lands End Trial of 1961.*

Yes, there was a time when they even raced Mini vans – this shot was taken in the early sixties.

Following impressive wins in the Tulip and Alpine rallies a particularly memorable event was the 1964 Monte Carlo rally, which was won by Paddy Hopkirk and Henry Liddon in 33 EJB.

There is apparently nothing special about this Mini being raced at Mallory Park in 1965 by Rod Embley, until you look closer at the air intake in the rear window. Yes, it is there to help cool a second engine. Furthermore, both engines in this car were rather special, being built by Gordon Allen, using specially cast blocks and Jaguar 2.4 heads with the middle two cylinders cut out to give four-cylinder designs. Combined output of the two units was 236 bhp at 6000 rpm.

Prepared by Ralph Broad, just before the great days of the Broadspeed team, this is Jeff May's 997 Cooper accelerating away from a Turner Sports at Silverstone in 1963.

Opposite: Displaying typical Mini understeer, Gordon Spice's Cooper 'S' holds off the similar cars of Tony Lanfranchi (44) and Harry Ratcliffe (43) at Crystal Palace in May 1966.

By 1965, when this shot was taken, the Mini Cooper was a much feared competitor in all major international rallies. This is the 1275 'S' of Paddy Hopkirk and Terry Harryman on the Circuit of Ireland event.

John Rhodes was one of the fastest ever Mini drivers. Here he is going very side-ways, very hard, having just passed Robertson's Nathan Imp in the 750 Motor Club's 6-hour Relay at Silverstone in August 1966.

David nibbles at the backside of Goliath—typically stirring saloon racing in the sixties, John Handley in the Mini.

It did not matter where the event was, there was generally a Mini to be seen somewhere in the thick of the action. This time it's Australia with the Cooper 'S' of Paddy Hopkirk and G. Chapman throwing up clouds of spray as it surges through a creek crossing near Wagga, New South Wales, during the 1966 Rothmans Southern Cross Rally.

Considering its origins, no-one could ever have dreamed that the old BMC A-series engine would turn into a hot, high performance world beater. This is how the Cooper 1275 'S' unit looked when prepared by BMC's Abingdon competitions department for rallies in 1966/67.

How to turn a Mini power unit into a plumber's nightmare, as demonstrated by Abingdon on one of the fuel injected 1275 'S' Coopers for the 1967 RAC Rally.

The big advantage for Minis in autocross was their front-wheel drive controllability. This is the car of Ian Thompson and Mick Bolton shown during a final in 1967. Photograph: Dave Gray

A special Mini-Moke event was held during the Players No. 6 National Autocross Championships at Studley Green, near High Wycombe in September 1967. Looks like it was a lot of fun!

More autocross, or is it a demolition derby?

After the previous year when a Mini had won the event, the 1968 Monte Carlo Rally provided a meagre third, fourth and fifth for the BMC works team. This is Tony Fall and Mike Wood's car.

Typical Mini action during a Special Saloon event at one of the Brands Hatch Mini Festivals in the late sixties – Simon Ridge spins and Robert Mandry takes avoiding action.

During the late sixties, ex-Team Broadspeed drivers John Handley and John Rhodes were driving for the Cooper Car Company team. This is Rhodes in classic overarm pose.

Amazing Mini

Alec Poole gained fame as a Mini racer with his Glaxo Laboratories-sponsored, turbocharged 1293cc Complan Mini. He is shown here successfully holding off Brian Muir's Camaro at Ingliston in October 1970. Photograph: Colin Lourie.

As they were developed to remain competitive in saloon racing, Minis acquired all sorts of unlikely power units. Pictured at Ingliston in August 1973, Sedric Bell's very rapid machine was propelled by an ex-Formula 3 1000cc Ford BDA motor. Photograph: Colin Lourie.

*Well known for his hairy and daredevil antics with Minis, which often resulted
in them getting written off, 'Jumping' Jeff Williamson is shown here driving
in typically enthusiastic style during a rallycross event in Denmark in 1971.
An eight-port crossflow head motor hides under the elegant bonnet.*

This sophisticated space frame chassis was one of the first ever built for a Mini racer. Completed in 1973, it was the work of Tony Chamings. With the Ford BDA engine mounted solidly to form part of the structure, the chassis was fabricated from a combination of $2\frac{1}{2}$ inch and $1\frac{1}{4}$ inch diameter steel tubing, with a $1\frac{1}{2}$ inch roll cage. The suspension was specially made, and the Mini body used panels of glassfibre, steel and aluminium.

The enterprising Gordon Allen built the very special 16 valve motor in this Mini, which was driven by Peter Kitchen at Silverstone in August 1974. The car performed so well that in practice it took pole position from the might of Frank Gardner's Camaro and Gerry Marshall's V8 Firenza.

Thanks to its regular successes, this machine soon became known amongst its competitors as 'That Bloody Van'! Featuring an all-aluminium monocoque chassis, an aluminium body, glassfibre roof, glassfibre bonnet, beam axle suspension and a 970cc Cooper engine, the car was built by specialist auto engineers Marshall and Fraser of Aylesbury in 1975. It is shown here at Mallory Park in 1976 with five-port 999cc Cooper power on its way to winning the B.A.R.C. Forward Trust 1000cc Championship.

Amazing Mini

Smallest vehicle in the 1977 Singapore Airlines Rally from London to Sydney was this Moke driven by Hans Tholstrup and John Crawford. Mad they might have been, but it just goes to prove you cannot keep a good Mini out of the action.

Monster Mini. Built by John Maguire of Coventry and using one of his well known space frame chassis, this evil looking machine was raced by Caerphilly driver Viv Wallace in 1978 and 1979. Power was courtesy of a 1000cc Arden engine with an 8-port head, special cam and twin Webers.

Richard Longman remained loyal to the Mini for many years, and crowned his long list of successes by winning Group 1 of the British Saloon Car Championship in 1978 and 1979. His 1275GT Mini is shown here at Donington Park in 1978.

Mini antics again, this time at the National Mini Championships at Castle Coombe.

Ah, that's the spirit. Having lost a wheel from his 1275GT at Paddock Bend, Brands Hatch, in 1979, John Mowatt did a complete lap of the long circuit on three wheels and a brake disc!

Chrysler Imp propulsion sits under the bonnet of John Flack's Mini shown here at Brands Hatch in 1979. Produced by Fibresports of Basildon, the Roadhog Mk.2 spoiler assembly is also fitted by many a road car customiser.

Hailed as the king of Mini racing in recent years, Peter Baldwin broke lap records and took class wins in virtually every race he entered in 1980. Shown here at Mallory Park, neck and neck with Derek Walker's 2-litre Cosworth-powered Skoda, Peter's car used a Reg Ward space frame chassis and the ex-Gordon Allen Ford BDA engine.

John Meredith's regular participation in hillclimb events since 1969 has earned him the dubious title 'The Old Man of the Hills'. Still, John does not mind as long as he can show the youngsters a thing or two–as he did by winning the RAC Hillclimb Championships in 1977 and 1979. Shown at Wiscombe Park in Devon, this was the 1979 car which was powered by a 985cc Chrysler Imp engine.

By 1980 John Meredith was running 'That Bloody Van', the ex-Marshall & Fraser Mini traveller. Rebuilt with a John Maguire space frame chassis, revised bodywork with aerodynamic additions and still running an Imp engine, the car is shown here at Wiscombe Park hillclimb on its way to another win.

5
Chic Mini

Conceived as the most basic and efficient of small cars in the late sixties, the Mini stumbled through its first couple of years in production with the customers at the end of the line not at all sure what to make of it. But the moment the car was turned into a fashionable object by the wealthy and trendy people of London, it never looked back. So it is a fact that the chic Mini, the luxury Mini, the prestige Mini, converted professionally, was the one Mini variant which contributed most to the basic model's eventual success.

That great car enthusiast, the late Peter Sellers, was probably the person who set the ball rolling. He had a Mini specially decked out with mock basketwork door panels and then set about publicising it in the way that only he knew how. That gave the little Mini a tremendous boost, and it was not surprising that others were quick to join the action. Just about the first company to become prominent in the field of Mini conversions was a London coachbuilding concern called Harold Radford Ltd. Radfords was part of the large Swain group of companies and, for some time had been tailoring to special order quality limousines like Rolls-Royces and Bentleys, but without really showing healthy enough profits. So when the Swain Group's managing director, P. F. Swain, and its marketing director, Graham Arnold, walked around the 1962 Motor Show together, they were specifically looking for a small car which Radfords could set to work on and thus revitalise their image as well as the car's.

In fact, the car Swain and Arnold chose initially was the Fiat 500, but this was soon discarded in favour of the Mini Cooper which had far more space and engine power. The car went down to Radford's Hammersmith workshops and on the counter appeared a range of 'goodies' with which to transform it: a Benelite grille with two extra spotlamps, Riley 1.5 headlamp cowls, a soundproofing kit, an electric window conversion, a Webasto sliding roof, a brand new facia and dashboard, several extra instruments, a wood-rimmed steering wheel, lambswool carpeting, leather for trimming, a radio and so on. Then, when the finished car sat in the middle of the workshop early in 1963, the press were informed and the reaction awaited. And what a reaction it turned out to be! Press and TV coverage were terrific: the era of the mini-

Rolls-Royce was under way.

First customer for a Radford Mini – three models were available in different stages of trim: the De-Ville, Bel-Air and Grande Luxe – was Basil Smallpiece, the chairman of Cunard, and soon the order book was filling fast. BMC were not particularly happy about it all, but there was little they could do for other companies were getting in on the act by now and producing some interesting variations on the theme. Rather than go luxury, Crayford Auto Development of Westerham, Kent, decided to go convertible, and it worked so well that film makers MGM were quickly on the telephone ordering a second example for use in *Night Must Fall*, starring Susan Hampshire and Albert Finney. After that, the Westerham company went on to build hundreds of convertible Minis, and still do to this day. The cost has risen a bit, of course, from about £150 to £1400!

Although Radford and Crayford were the most prominent names back in the very early days of Mini limousines, the most famous name today is that of Wood & Pickett. In fact, Bill Wood and Les Pickett built their first chic Mini – a £1000 job for actress Hayley Mills – not long after Radfords had begun making a name for themselves, but somehow never quite gained the same publicity and acclaim until some time later. However, by 1967/68 Margrave Minis (Margrave was Wood & Pickett's brand name) were looking particularly fine with rectangular headlamps which distinguished them from the otherwise similarly equipped Radford cars.

Following sales of Margrave Minis to many of the world's leading celebrities, Wood & Pickett's business reached a peak during the 1973/74 oil crisis when the company's established Rolls-Royce and Bentley customers turned towards more economical transport and, in particular, luxury Minis. By the late seventies there was so much Arab oil money around that it was not unknown for the occasional Margrave to be worth anything between £10,000 and £20,000! Certainly the £10,000 car was no rarity, enjoying amongst its vast range of creature comforts such items as a radio telephone, electrically operated sun roof, opening rear door, colour television and air conditioning. Today, with petrol becoming more and more expensive, Wood & Pickett are finding their Mini conversions still as popular as ever and, with about 800 cars built to date, it surely will not be long before the magical 1000 is reached.

Away from all the glamour and showbiz razzmatazz of Radford and Wood & Pickett, two other very different chic Minis are worthy of note – the supersmooth Mini-Sprint and the fastback Broadspeed GT, both appearing in 1966. Designed by Neville Trickett, the Mini-Sprint was clever in that it took all the stodginess out of the Mini's styling and transformed it into a highly attractive and very desirable little 'blob'. To start with, the job was done by removing the body seams and chopping $1\frac{1}{2}$ inches from the windscreen

WOLSELEY *Hornet* **Mk II**

with Hydrolastic Suspension

Above: *Economy and elegance. The Wolseley Hornet, and to a greater extent the Riley Elf, added luxury to the basic car. Shown here is a 1964 Catalogue*

Below: *The interior of the Elf MK.III. (Graham Thompson)*

The Mini Moke, pictured in suitably 'off-road' conditions. (Chris Harvey)

Above: *The 1000cc basic model for 1983, the Mini City.*

Below: *Specifications for the 1984 Mayfair included built-in head rests, cut-pile carpets, a radio and tinted windows.*

Above: *The Mini has achieved brilliant success in many forms of motor sport. Here a pack of rallycross Minis enter the Esses at Brands Hatch. (Chris Harvey)*

Below: *The Mini of Mick Hill, minicross champion in 1982. (Trevor Hill)*

and window pillars plus another $1\frac{1}{2}$ inches from the body below its waistline. Then, after the first batch of cars had been built, several variations appeared and customers could order cars with rectangular headlamps, no rain channels and so on. They looked superb, and the company which marketed Trickett's work, G. T. Equipment Company of Poole, Dorset, found many keen customers, Stirling Moss being one. But after only a year of production, the Mini-Sprint project was bought by BMC distributors, Stewart and Ardern, and after that things were never the same again. In fact, the Mini-Sprint more or less disappeared completely.

As for the Broadspeed GT, this was a miniature GT car which aimed to combine a Mini with an Aston Martin. Ralph Broad, famous more recently for his work with the BL racing Jaguars, took a brand new Mini body shell, removed the roof, rear bodywork and windscreen, and attached a new fast-back rear body and roof moulding which linked up with a new windscreen. The end result was a lower, longer Mini which had luxury trim and cost around £1400 with a 1000cc Cooper engine. It was certainly an attractive package but, like so many specialist projects, went to the great scrapyard in the sky after about 28 cars had been built.

Behind all the big names in the chic Mini business came a variety of small operations offering special glassfibre front ends (no-one was ever quite certain about the legality of these) and grille conversions. Few ever lasted very long but at least they demonstrated how great was enthusiasm for the little old Mini–and still is to this day. Perhaps the strangest aspect of the whole thing is that BMC or BL never got involved with a true luxury Mini. The nearest they ever came was with the Cooper Car Company's Bertone Mini Cooper 'S' VIP, a car which was shipped to Italy in 1966 for the master coachbuilder to give it an oh-so-subtle prestige treatment. But sad to say, only one example was ever built.

Today, as already stated, Wood & Pickett are the masters of the chic Mini art. But other companies are quietly creeping into the business, and it looks very much as though this particular variety of the amazing Mini still has loads of life left in it yet.

The very first professionally built 'luxury' Minis came from Harold Radford & Company Ltd. This early Radford car is pictured at BMC's Longbridge factory in 1963 where engineers were running an eye over its modifications – wind-down windows, re-styled dashboard, re-trimmed seats, cowled headlamps, sun roof, wheel trims and imitation basketwork side panels.

Opposite: *Thanks to all the extra weight, most of Harold Radford's cars were built from Mini Coopers – standard cars were not powerful enough to cope! Known as the Radford Mini Grande Luxe, this was the ultimate interior in 1963, featuring electric windows, leather trim, lambswool carpeting, veneered wood dashboard with glove locker, extra instruments and a wood-rim steering wheel.*

Amazing Mini

Crayford Auto Development of Westerham, Kent, was another company in at the start of the Mini conversion business and specialised in open top versions. Built in 1963, this was Crayford's very first car. The ugly auxiliary light panel was made of glassfibre and the whole conversion cost around £150 depending on final specification.

Styled by BMC's chief stylist, Dick Burzi, this beach car went into limited production at Longbridge around the same time as the first Crayford and Radford cars appeared. And 'limited' was the right word too, for less than 20 examples were built in all.

Bottom left: *Another Crayford conversion, this time on a Wolseley Hornet. Hundreds of Minis have been 'opened-up' at Westerham over the years, and the company still receives regular orders to this day.*

133

Wood & Pickett was another London coachbuilding company which turned its hand from Rolls-Royces to Minis. This early example of the company's work is based on a Riley Elf and is most notable for its neat headlamp conversion.

Opposite, top: *Although one example is known to remain in Britain, most of the beach car Minis went abroad to more suitable climates. Hotels were the chief customers, using the cars to ferry guests from bar to beach.*

Opposite, bottom: *First man to think of cutting the Mini bodyshell down to give a smoother appearance was Mini racing driver Neville Trickett. Built by the G. T. Equipment Company of Poole, Dorset, Trickett's design was called the Mini-Sprint and was introduced early in 1966. While the first cars retained circular headlamps, Trickett soon moved on to rectangular units. Mini-Sprints were built to customers' individual requirements–hence these two cars have noticeable differences.*

134

Amazing Mini

Opposite: *Perhaps the smoothest of all Minis, the Mini-Sprint conversion involved cutting and lowering the body both above and below the waistline. Towards the end of 1966, production rights for the car were bought by BMC distributors, Stewart and Ardern, but strangely enough things gradually petered out after that.*

Not content with building Mini convertibles, Crayford also had a go at the Moke, and produced about 20 of these Surrey Mokes for customers in the Caribbean and the South of France. One was also used in the TV series 'The Prisoner', starring Patrick McGoohan.

Probably one of the first Minis to feature an opening rear door was the special Radford Mini de Ville GT given by Peter Sellers to his wife Britt Eckland in October 1965. The whole of the rear body panel was a special glassfibre moulding

incorporating a steel hoop to provide rigidity and act as the attachment point for the door hinges.

With Radford, Wood & Pickett and Crayford all hard at work perfecting the Mini, it was not surprising that the development engineers at Longbridge also decided to have a go. This car was built for the Minister of Transport, Ernest Marples.

Opposite: *Following Team Ridgway's success with George Lawrence's streamlined racing Cooper 'S', this smart conversion was offered for public consumption late in 1966. Costing only £24 and known as the Ridgway Sports Conversion, the kit comprised a glassfibre bonnet, a special plastic grille and a glassfibre nose which was attached by eight self-tapping screws.*

The Mini Festival at Brands Hatch in 1968 produced a terrific selection of Mini variants. The cars on the left and right of the front row are luxury Margrave Minis built by Wood & Pickett.

Also at the Brands Hatch Mini Festival was this unusual convertible. Its exact origins are unknown but it was probably the work of development engineers at Longbridge.

The idea behind the Broadspeed GT was to produce a combination of Aston Martin style and comfort with Mini Cooper 'S' performance, economy and practicality. About 28 cars were built at Ralph Broad's Birmingham workshops between 1966 and 1968.

Opposite: *In 1971, prestige car specialists, Guy Salmon Ltd., asked a Thames Ditton coachbuilder to build this Mini special with a view to putting the model into limited production. Unfortunately, only the one car was ever completed, although other less radical Minis were made to order.*

146

This mock Rolls-Royce grille was not really such a bad idea. Designed by ex-Lotus man, Brian Luff, the glassfibre conversion found about 30 willing customers in 1971 before Rolls-Royce Motors created a stink and forced Luff to stop production.

Opposite: *The Cuda Mini conversion was offered by a company called Woodway Studios of Coventry early in 1973. Costing £21.50, it comprised two glassfibre mouldings which simply fitted over the bonnet-less standard Mini bodywork. Also available was another moulding which transformed and extended the Mini's rear end.*

And this is what a Wood & Pickett interior looks like. Features include Dralon trimmed seats, leather trimmed facia, veneered wood dashboard and a fine array of instruments and switches.

Wood & Pickett again, and this time it's a car showing the company's clever use of a proprietary headlamp/radiator grille panel. Recognise it? Yes, it's a Vauxhall Ventora unit.

With most of the competition no longer in existence, by the mid-1970's Wood &
Pickett's North London factory was undoubtedly the place to go for coachbuilt

152

Minis. Here, managing director Eddie Collins and his staff pose with some of their products.

153

Perhaps the best looking and most suitable of all headlamp conversions applied to the Mini was this Mercedes transplant carried out by Wood & Pickett. This really is an ace looking Mini.

Opposite: *Offered by Redbird Design of South Benfleet, Essex, in 1975, the Redbird Mini front end conversion cost £39.90 and included a pair of matching rear wheel arch extensions. Only a small number were made.*

Overleaf: *Typical of Wood & Pickett's work in 1976 was this Mini conversion which took around 12 weeks and raised the car's value to about £6500. Apart from the obvious external modifications, the interior was naturally uprated to match.*

154

Amazing Mini

Having reached a peak during the 1973/74 oil crisis and then quietened down in favour of cars like the Range Rover, Wood & Pickett's Mini conversion work has recently become more popular again thanks to petrol's continually rising price. This one is neat.

Top left: *It might look rather like a Wood & Pickett car, but this is actually a Trevor James Mini as supplied in the late 1970's by Trevor James Car Conversions of St. Alban's, Hertfordshire. James' idea was to do a full Wood & Pickett style conversion to the car's body and interior but at something less than half the cost.*

Bottom left: *Perhaps the most recent entry to the Mini conversion field is a company called Automobilia. Based in North London, Automobilia offer Wood & Pickett style work at more affordable prices, this Phaeton Mini costing around £3500 and being built on a late but second-hand base car.*

159

6
Custom Mini

While professional customisers and coachbuilders have never been short of ideas for up-grading the basic Mini concept, they have always treated the car with a certain respect; in other words they have kept to the more refined end of the personalisation business. The real D.I.Y. customiser, however, is another breed again, and is likely to stretch the meaning of the word 'customise' to the furthest possible limits. The custom world is a world where anything is possible . . .

It all started fairly innocently. With superb roadholding and sprightly performance available to the public at large, people fell in love with their Minis right from the start and were naturally keen to add those little personal touches that made their car just that fraction 'better' than the one next door. The personal touch took the form of items like sun visors, wheel spacers, wheel spats, wide alloy wheels, mud flaps or stick-on side stripes. If the job was to be done really nicely then it needed a special custom radiator grille, some extra lights and a special paint scheme. Interiors were not forgotten, either, many Mini fans re-working their dashboards and generally making big efforts to turn their spartan little boxes into comfortable, homely carriages. But all this was really just the tip of the rainbow.

Apart from all the flower-power paint jobs and the shortened, lengthened and double-fronted 'silly' Minis (which will be covered in the forthcoming companion volume to this book), the first really radical custom Minis were the individually modified chop-tops which followed the Mini-Sprint theme devised by Neville Trickett. Often with their rain channels and body seams removed, these well rounded 'blobs' began to appear in small numbers from mid-1966 onwards, and signalled the start of an all-out blitz on the poor unsuspecting Mini. There were aluminium body mods, glassfibre body mods, headlamp conversions and radiators grafted on from other cars. There were six-wheelers, flat bed trucks, convertibles and luxury vans. There were spoilers, wings, murals and goodness knows what; and despite the growing tendency of the average custom builder to get more and more outrageous, there were still the subtle jobs—replicas of the old works racers, for instance, or clean simple estates converted from vans.

Amazing Mini

Perhaps the most surprising thing about the custom Mini is that it has never gone out of favour. With the custom business having grown enormously over 20 years, one could be forgiven for wondering why customisers have not moved on to greater things. However, they still love the Mini, and no doubt will go on loving it for years yet. What have they got in store that has not been tried already? Well, there is an eight-wheeler Mini for a start . . .

Early customising was not quite the same as we know it now! This early Mini displays some of the dealer-fitted options which presumably were thought, at the time, to make the car that little bit 'snazzier'. The roof rack was also useful for carrying luggage.

This Mini shows one line of custom thinking back in the early sixties, sporting a sunroof, boot-mounted spare and special dashboard. The man responsible was Sandy Fraser, who went on to build the Mini-powered AF Spyder and Grand Prix described later in this book.

No Mini variant was to escape the clutches of the customiser. This Countryman has been 'worked over' with wicker – not such a bad treatment after all.

Whether you could really call this a custom job or not is very much open to question! Certainly the Moke's appearance was hardly enhanced when lumbered with this glassfibre hardtop sold for £133 by Dick Barton Ltd. of Plymouth during the mid-sixties.

Shown at one of the Brands Hatch Mini Festivals of 1967/68, these three Minis have all undergone roof chops. It was an idea which started with the professionally built Mini-Sprint early in 1966 and soon blossomed amongst D.I.Y. enthusiasts.

Thankfully, not too many people followed **Hot Car** magazine's example. This smart six-wheel Mini truck shows the real way to go about customising. Built by Mini racing specialists Howley Racing of Warrington, Lancs., it started life as a Mini van and grew up with glassfibre front bodywork, a Mini Cooper 'S' 1400 cc engine, Mini pick-up rear bodywork and a special frame for the extra pair of wheels.

*Er . . . yes, well . . . what can one say! This motorised Christmas tree, splattered with a £300 avalanche of bolt-on, stick-on and thrown-on cosmetic horrors, was the project vehicle which helped launch **Hot Car** magazine early in 1968. It was a superb example of just how badly a car could be customised.*

One man's ideal Mini–Gerry Bath of Upper Swainswick, near Bath, felt that the best all-round Mini consisted of a Mini van with Perspex side windows, Hydrolastic Cooper 'S' subframes, a breathed-on MG1100 engine and a single rear door hinged at the top, so that was exactly what he built. For good measure he revised the front styling with new aluminium panels.

During the early seventies, enthusiasts were trying all sorts of approaches to individualising their Minis. This car has a special grille and twin Humber headlamp units.

This modification is so neat it's surprising that BLMC never got round to trying it – Riley Elf with square headlamps.

The 'blob' look! This car started life as a standard Mini, was 'de-seamed' and then had $4\frac{3}{4}$ inches chopped out of its window pillars, and it looks good.

Proud owner with another 'chopped' Mini. The difference between privately modified cars and professionally built Mini-Sprints was often that the latter were chopped below the waistline as well as above, thus rectifying the unbalanced appearance of this car.

Opposite: *This Mini was just about ready for the scrapyard when it was rebuilt into a very smooth luxury car. De-seaming, a vinyl roof and wheel spats were the major exterior modifications.*

While the professionals were charging hundreds or thousands of pounds, enthusiasts were doing similar jobs on a shoestring. This interior has been

172

transformed with a wood-framed, leather-trimmed dashboard, Jaguar gauges and switches, and Rover seats.

There is nothing particularly special about this car, but it does show how a little attention can turn a Mini van into a tidy estate at minimum cost.

Looking like an out-and-out racer, which it almost was with 1320 cc Cooper 'S' power, this machine was built up from a standard Clubman. Lowered suspension, wide wheels and racing tyres with specially cut treads all added to the character.

Practical customising, obviously not done with a view to winning any prizes but certainly useful for carrying things like the trials bike or the mother-in-law.

Ah, that's rather classy. Goodness knows what Mercedes would say, though they certainly would not have approved of that bit of wire holding the number plate on! Photograph: Mike Key.

Good customisers show no fear. This car started life as a 1961 Mini van and the modifications were started by the driver of a Ford. The front bodywork was developed from an off-the-shelf glassfibre moulding.

Apart from fitting side windows, many Mini van owners used to replace the twin rear doors with a special single door sold by companies like Intertech. This improved visibility.

The 'works' look. One of the first 400 Minis off the production line in 1959, this immaculate machine was rebuilt in the mid-seventies by a Scottish enthusiast. Amazingly enough, corrosion was so minimal that only the front wings and front apron needed replacement. The 12 × 8 Minilite wheels were from an ex-BLMC works racer. Photograph: Peter Hingston.

The point about customising is that for a lot of work and relatively little outlay you can end up with something very special. Bolton man John Buckley's ultra-smooth Mini started out as a bare shell of 1964 vintage. Some hundreds of hours later it had undergone a total transformation and had become just about the most refined custom Mini in the country.

Another van, but this time left as a van and given a rather unsuitable and flowery paint job. Still, dating from the late seventies, it just shows how even

*the most basic Mini variant has remained very much in favour with the custom
brigade. Photograph: Mike Key.*

Pick-me-up for a pick-up – special paint, murals, tinted windows, shovel spoiler, twin headlamp units, alloy wheels and the whole works!

Opposite: The chopped roof, de-seamed Mini-Sprint look is probably the classic amongst Mini conversions, and is still being practised even now. This little smoothie was completed in 1978 by High Wycombe man Bob Hollingsworth. It took him 2500 hours – over no less than three years!

Mike Chaplin of Colchester operates a specialist Mini garage and has built these two variations on the theme. Notice how the boot-mounted spare wheel on the saloon goes back to the very earliest days of Mini customising. The truck is 17 ft. long and was built from a 1966 pick-up saved from the scrappers.

After the last photograph, this car represents exactly the opposite approach. Called 'That Mini', it's wild, exaggerated and outrageous. Built up from a basic 1978 body shell over 18 months, it was finally finished in mid-1979 at a total cost of around £2500. Since then it has been a regular prizewinner at custom shows.

Opposite: The interior of 'That Mini' is as wild as its exterior. It includes brass buttoned gold Dralon upholstery, home-made front seats, home-made dash and console, electric windows and a steering wheel made from an alloy road wheel!

This six-wheeler pick-up started life as an ex-RAC van bought for £70. It was then cut in half and mated with a Mini pick-up bought from a scrapyard. When Southampton man Terry Cooper finished the job in mid-1979, he had only spent £700 in total.

Mild custom Mini for the man about town. This 1275GT has only had nudge bars and a vinyl roof added, but it's just enough to give a spot of 'class'.

Opposite: *Bob Hollingsworth's masterpiece grew from a '76 Clubman shell with a damaged roof. A new roof was fitted, 5 inches were taken from the screen pillars and 5 more inches from the body below its waistline. The interior and 1300 cc engine were also given the full treatment.*

184

7
Alternative Mini

Alec Issigonis, Jack Daniels and the rest of the BMC development engineers working on the Mini at Longbridge during the late 1950's realised that they had on their hands a concept which offered endless opportunity for derivatives. However, even they could have had little idea how far the one basic layout could be stretched, or how long it would go on being stretched!

The whole idea of alternative or special-bodied Minis had a lot to do with the great character of the standard Mini. What could be fun, rapid and economical in a heavy steel bodyshell could surely be several degrees better in a lightweight glassfibre-bodied structure. True, it was likely to offer less passenger space, but who worried about that when the alternative Mini represented total individuality and perhaps the chance to own an exotic looker at an affordable price; plus, it was a fine opportunity to re-cycle the still serviceable running gear from a crashed or badly rusting Mini.

Generally sold in kit form for home completion–this way the builder saved Purchase Tax, at least until 1973–the alternative Mini made a lot of sense, and still does. Whatever might happen to a basic Mini, it has always been likely that the engine/transmission and suspension package, all mounted on its own easily removable subframe, will still be worth saving. Indeed, both this front end assembly and the rear subframe assembly have always been easily available as brand new components or spares off-the-shelf at any suitable dealer. Old or new, it has never mattered, the point being that the Mini's ingenious running gear assemblies have always been ideal for use by specialist manufacturers in 'alternative' bodies. For years now, operating around the basis of the little old Mini, there has been a vast, varied and extremely interesting industry.

With BMC building their first Mini derivatives early in 1960 only a few months after the Mini saloon's launch, it was only natural that would-be specialist manufacturers should take a little longer to allow themselves time for development. But it was not much longer, because in January 1962 at the Racing Car Show in London, were the first two alternative Minis ever! In truth, the front-engined Butterfield Musketeer and rear-engined Deep Sanderson Type 301 were both rather under-developed, because the former

187

was not ready for production until much later in 1962, by which time the initial interest had dwindled away, and the latter was also very much a proto- type. But between them they showed what was possible, and that was the important thing.

The alternative Mini business became an intriguing one because its products were so surprising and innovative, and because it could switch so quickly from a thriving situation to a barely surviving one. Of course, many companies just did not make it, and bankruptcy was a word which quickly became associated with the whole idea of specialist cars. For the sixties though, most manufacturers of special-bodied Minis kept things fairly cool. The really suicidal stuff was to come later.

The sixties trend was straightforward glassfibre-bodied sports cars, mostly front-engined and mostly two-seaters with a little room in the back. No-one was too bothered about practicality, although there were exceptions: the Ogle Mini was a very professionally made 2 +2 sports saloon and the Uni- power GT was a superbly engineered mid-engined sports car with a terrific combination of performance, handling and roadholding. Indeed, of all the alternative Minis of the 1960's, it is these two cars alone that are considered collectable.

By the end of the 1960's, the specialist and kit car business had established a very strong market for pure fun cars, and alternative Minis were of course in the thick of it. Following the demise of the Mini Moke in 1968, everybody suddenly wanted basic open runabouts–for daily utility work, for laughs on the beach and simply to be non-conformist. Designed and built by Surrey farmer, Robert Mandry, the Mini-Scamp was to become the best known Mini-based fun car, though Neville Trickett and Barry Stimson were not far behind with their ideas. Trickett designed only two Mini funsters, the Siva Mule and Siva Buggy, but Stimson came up with a whole string of them, each one a very individual piece of thinking and the best one probably being the attractive Safari Six.

While the fun car boom continued strongly during the early 1970's, by 1973 it was steadily weakening and rendering itself helpless to fight the drastic effects of VAT. Indeed, the alternative Mini market suffered badly from this evil bureaucratic taxation scheme, because people could no longer save Purchase Tax by building their own car from a kit. Still, the remnants of the business struggled on and created a diverse and haphazard pattern for the rest of that decade. Alternative Minis had never been quite as 'alter- native' before! There were thirties-style three-wheeler ones, four-wheel motorbike ones, very short silly ones, three-wheeler silly ones and even the odd leftover from the fun car boom. Of course, there were also the occasional sensible ones, and these were the cars which were pointing the way ahead for the next generation of alternative Minis.

The people who built specialist and kit cars during the 1960's had sold them to make way for the family, buying 'sensible' steel cars. Then they got fed up with all the rust and the end of the 1970's showed that alternative Minis were once again extremely popular as long as they were practical, professionally finished and came close to matching the high overall standards of mass-production cars. Undoubted leader of the current pack is the superb Midas, very much a car for the 1980's. Apart from being designed by Richard Oakes, a professional automotive stylist, and thus having a neat, modern appearance, it offers excellent 2 +2 accommodation, very economic running costs, a very high standard of finish and, most important of all, a 100% guarantee that its main body/chassis structure will never go rusty. And slaving away under the bonnet, still giving good performance, is the ubiquitous Mini engine.

Another trend-setter amongst current alternative Minis is the stylish Hustler, a sort of modern Moke. Like the Midas, the Hustler offers a 'total' package–it was professionally styled by Aston Martin Lagonda man, William Towns; it is economical, it will take a lot of bad weather to get it decomposing, and it offers room for at least four adults. But the extraordinary thing about the Minis described in this chapter is that they are still happening–refusing to die. The very aptly named Phoenix is the latest, a sort of modern Mini Countryman, its glassfibre and plywood monocoque structure again offering the best non-rust certificate in the business.

As a final comment on alternative Minis, it could well be argued that the Midas, Hustler and Phoenix are all much better equipped motor cars than the standard Mini. But what a great tribute it is to the Mini's mechanical assemblies that they can still do such a good job some 22 years after they were first made available to the public. Moreover, judging by the fact that even more Mini-based specialist car projects are under way, there is still plenty of life left in them yet.

Swashbuckling Mini. The Butterfield Musketeer was built during 1961 and announced at the January 1962 Racing Car Show. It was offered in complete component form with either the Mini 850 or Mini Cooper 997 engine, prices being £850 and £892 respectively. But despite the obvious desirability of an individual and non-rust glassfibre-bodied Mini, the public preferred the ones that rusted. Only three Musketeers were built.

Opposite: *The first specialist manufacturer to see the potential in mounting the Mini engine at the rear of a low-slung sports car was Chris Lawrence. Known as the Deep Sanderson Type 301, the car made its debut at the Racing Car Show in January 1962. It is seen here being driven by Len Bridge at a Biggin Hill Sprint meeting in April the same year.*

Mini metamorphosis. Announced early in 1962, the Ogle Mini was the first serious attempt at re-bodying the Mini by a British company. Carried out by David Ogle Ltd. of Letchworth, the conversion involved stripping a Mini saloon down to its platform (all running gear was left intact), adding rigidity by welding on new side members and then re-clothing the assembly with a one-piece glassfibre body. The end result was a more individual and durable Mini which soon raised a few eyebrows at BMC! With probably less than 50 examples in existence, the car is nowadays something of a collector's item.

Opposite: *By 1963 the unorthodox shape of the Deep Sanderson Type 301 open prototype had been transformed into the smoothly attractive 301 fastback coupe of which a small quantity were sold in kit form. The only Mini parts used on the car were the engine, hubs and wheels, the special Lawrence-Link trailing arm suspension system being hung from a substantial steel backbone and box-section chassis. For access to the engine, the whole rear half of the glassfibre body tilted backwards.*

*Apart from racing Mini saloons, John Handley also had a go in several altern-
ative Minis. He is seen here at Castle Coombe in August 1966 cornering
hard in a modified 1149 cc Cooper-Nosy Mini. Developed from a 1964 one-off
Mini special called the Dart, the Mini-Marcos slipped on to the market in 1965.*

For £199, the customer received a fibreglass and plywood monocoque body/ chassis unit which re-cycled the sub-frames and all running gear from a rusting or crashed Mini. It might have looked a little ungainly with its high bonnet and low rear end, but over 1,000 examples of the Mini-Marcos have been sold.

Alternative Mini

Nowadays manufactured by D & H Fibreglass Techniques of Oldham, the Mini-Marcos has had an exceptionally long production run; and when you look at its attributes, this is hardly surprising. Apart from having an opening tailgate and 2+2 accommodation, the car is light, economical, lively and totally rust-proof in every area apart from its Mini subframes.

Opposite: *Mini Miura. Most attractive and desirable of all the Mini powered specialist cars, the Unipower GT was launched at the January 1966 Racing Car Show. Based around an independently suspended spaceframe chassis, the body was moulded to very high standards and smartly trimmed inside. Prices for complete kits with rear mounted Mini-Cooper 'S' engines were around the £1,000 mark. The finished item weighs some 4 cwt less than a standard Cooper 'S'. so it certainly does not hang around! Seventy-five cars were built before production ceased at the end of 1969. They are now much treasured collectors' items.*

Mighty Mini. It is Le Mans 1966 and what, you might be thinking, has this got to do with Minis? The answer lies with the second to last car in this pack tackling Mulsanne Corner – it is the 1275 Cooper 'S'-powered Mini Marcos

which was the first British car to finish the race that year. Driven by two French-men, the car finished in 15th position having averaged 89.63mph. Top speed down the Mulsanne straight was 130mph.

Thanks to the tilting rear body section, access to the Unipower GT's Mini Cooper engine was remarkably good. A complex gearchange linkage ended with a stubby gearstick mounted on the driver's door sill, and worked surprisingly efficiently.

Opposite: *Ugly Mini. Another 1966 Racing Car Show debutant, the Peel Viking Sport was not the prettiest of alternative Minis but did have durability and 2 +2 practicality on its side. Using moulded replicas of cut-down Mini doors, the glassfibre monocoque bodyshell sold for £230 and accepted standard Mini front and rear subframes. About 25 examples are thought to have been built by Peel Engineering on the Isle of Man before production ended in the late sixties.*

First appearing in 1966, the Camber GT was perhaps most notable for its unorthodox lines and illegally positioned headlamps! The car was the brainchild of George Holmes who ran a small garage on Camber Sands in Sussex. Beneath its fibreglass monocoque body (with tubular steel stiffening), it used standard Mini subframes front and rear. After about a year, and with only half a dozen or so cars built, Holmes restyled the front end to bring the headlamps to the correct height, and changed the car's name to Maya GT.

Opposite: *Showing off its Mini engine, this car is a Maya GT. It is thought only six examples had been completed by the time the car's designer George Holmes was tragically killed in a road accident.*

Midi Mini. If you had £330 and a rusting or smashed Mini in 1967, one fairly complicated way of converting it into a neat little mid-engined sports car was with the Cox GTM body/chassis unit offered by Bernard Cox's garage at Hazel Grove, Cheshire. The problem was caused by the amount of modification work required to the two Mini front subframes before they worked properly with the steel box-section chassis to produce reasonable standards of handling and roadholding. Even so, the car sold well and, in a much refined form, is still available today.

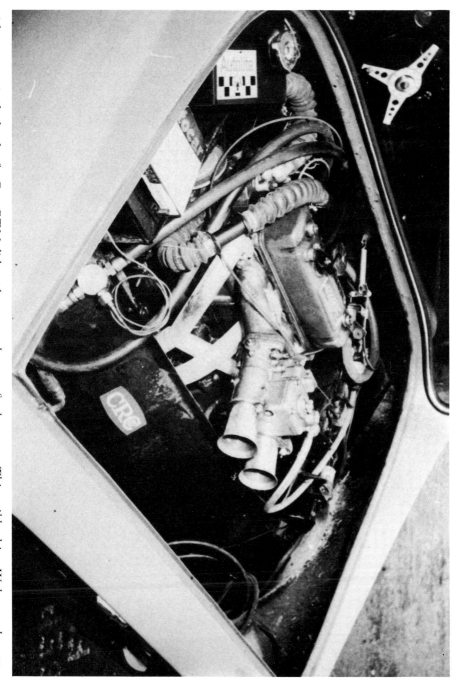

A hot motor in the back of a Cox GTM did not leave much room for luggage. This evil looking Weber carburettor has efficiently eliminated the car's luggage boot—which should have tucked tidily into the tail.

This is how the GTM looks today–a thoroughly modern Mini-powered, mid-engined machine giving few hints of its age. The price has gone up a bit mind you–to a basic £1250 plus VAT–but the car's continued appeal simply

proves how well the concept and running gear have aged. Current manufacturers are GTM Engineering of Nottingham.

Mini power pack in Mini Jem—a tight fit but still leaving excellent access. Several hundred Mini Jems were built by the three different companies who owned the project at one time or another, production finally grinding to a halt in 1975.

208

Another of 1967's opportunities for the alternative Mini enthusiast was the Fletcher GT. It was of course a modified version of the earlier Ogle Mini but, unlike the Ogle, was offered in kit form. This did not change its fortunes much because the manufacturers, Norman Fletcher Ltd. of Walsall, are believed to have only ever built four examples.

Overleaf: *Smoothie Mini. 1967 was a particularly good year for Mini-based kit cars. This little blob is a Mini Jem, which made its public debut early that year. Its fibreglass monocoque structure used standard Mini subframes front and rear, and shared its ancestry with the Mini-Marcos—hence the styling similarities.*

The Yak utility wagon neatly timed its arrival on the British market to coincide with the demise of the Mini Moke. Devised by two ex-TVR men, Bernard Williams and John Ward, the car's structure involved a tubular chassis, fibreglass bodywork and Mini subframes front and rear. About 150 body/chassis kits were sold before production ceased in 1973.

Opposite: *Hung at the front end of the Biota's tubular chassis was a complete Mini engine/subframe package. The rear suspension featured Mini trailing arms working in conjunction with coil spring/shock absorber units.*

If the Mini power unit was good enough for GT cars and utility wagons, then it was also good enough for a poor man's Lotus 7 – so thought racing driver John Houghton. And quite right he proved to be, for the Biota's combination of lightweight fibreglass body over Mini running gear added up to a very lively little roadburner. However, after a 1969 launch, only 30 or so kits were sold before the Biota faded away in the mid-seventies.

See-through Mini. Called the Quasar-Unipower, this amazing Mini-powered machine was built in 1968 by the same workforce that produced the very different Unipower GT. It followed the design of a French company director who wanted several examples for publicity use, and used a widened Mini subframe at each end. The power unit featured automatic transmission and was fitted underneath the rear seats. About half a dozen Quasars were built in total; most of them were sent abroad.

Opposite: Trimini. Using a glassfibre replica Mini front end, a complete Mini front subframe plus a modified and stiffened Mini floorpan with a single wheel to prop it up at the rear, the ABC Tricar was produced by Auto Bodycraft of Brierley Hill, Staffordshire. Priced from £400 ready to drive away, about 25 Tricars were built between 1969 and 1973.

Amazing Mini

Antique Mini. Making a refreshing change from all the buggies and utilities which made up the fun car boom of the early 1970's was this traditional three-wheeler called an AB1. Its construction involved a marine ply monocoque chassis with a complete Mini subframe at the front, while at the rear was a special tubular steel subframe for the trailing arm with coil spring/damper rear suspension. Designed by Sandy Fraser, the body was marine ply over a teak frame. AB1 body/chassis units were offered for sale by Antique Automobiles of Peterborough at prices from £275.

Top left: *The story behind this all-glassfibre Mini estate is that it was built by the famous Marcos company in 1969 on behalf of Autocars of Haifa, Israel, a company partly owned by BMC. Drawing on all their experience gained with the Mini-Marcos, the Marcos development men used a glassfibre monocoque body structure with a Mini windscreen and Clubman-type doors. Five examples were built including one 'fastback' derivative.*

Bottom left: *This is the 'fastback' estate prototype built by Marcos Cars for Autocars of Haifa. Despite thorough development including crash-testing, the project came to a halt when BMC sold their shareholding in Autocars. This particular car eventually went to the U.S.A. for conversion to electric power.*

217

With an all-up weight of only 8 cwt, the Stimson Mini Bug was a lively performer whatever Mini engine it used. Seen taking full advantage of the little machine's superb handling and roadholding, this is Vince Gonelli racing on the stock car circuit at Cowdenbeath in Scotland.

Top left: *Following the Min-Moke's despatch to Australia in 1968, there was a big gap on the market for a Mini utility. Designed by Robert Mandry, the Mini-Scamp first appeared in 1970 and went on to sell over 1,000 examples in kit form for home construction with two Mini subframes. Aluminium panels clothed the multi-tubular chassis, and so versatile was the Mini-Scamp's construction that it was available as a van, estate, pick-up, six-wheeler or ultra-short wheelbase fun car.*

Bottom left: *As if the number of Mini-based variants was not already getting out of hand by 1970, that year saw the Stimson Mini Bug awarded the dubious title of 'first ever Mini-based buggy'. While the front end was standard Mini, the rear suspension used Mini trailing arms and motorcycle coil spring/damper units. Designed by Barry Stimson—that's him in the cockpit—the Mini Bug was sold as a body/chassis kit for £170, and found about twenty customers.*

219

Announced in August 1970, the Siva Buggy was the first traditionally styled beach buggy to use Mini running gear – and also the last! Another Neville Trickett creation, the car was sold as a body/chassis unit for £195 and ran its two Mini subframes on 13 inch wheels. Almost 100 examples were sold before the end of the road in 1976.

Opposite: *Another utility Mini was the glassfibre-bodied Siva Mule of 1970. Designed by Neville Trickett, the Mule used a tubular steel chassis carrying Mini subframes front and rear. Although kits could be bought from the Siva company's workshop at Bryanston, Dorset, at prices from as low as £195, the Mule's production run was limited to about a dozen units.*

220

Unveiled at the Racing Car Show in January 1971, Barry Stimson's Mini Bug 2 was a fair improvement over his earlier effort–so much so that even British Leyland thought it was worth borrowing for a week for evaluation purposes. About 160 examples were built before production ended in 1973.

Opposite: *Tichy Mini. Designed by Anthony Hill, the TiCi was said at the time to be the shortest road car ever. Unfortunately, despite the backing of Stirling Moss, it also had rather a short production run, starting at the end of 1971 and ending two years later. A complete Mini engine and front subframe unit were mounted just behind the seats. The front suspension used Mini links and coil spring/damper units.*

222

Following its great success in its native Australia, where English born designer, Guy Buckingham, had sold lots of ready-to-go examples, the Nota Fang was introduced in the U.K. early in 1972 . . . and met with a resounding thud! Of fairly sophisticated chassis design, the Fang was offered as a complete body/ chassis unit needing only a Mini engine and subframe to be installed at the rear, but it seems no more than two or three cars were ever built here.

Top left: *By late 1971 the ABI had been developed into the improved AF Spider and designer Sandy Fraser had formed his own company to produce the car. A small number of Spiders was sold before Fraser produced this car, the Grand Prix, still using similar construction methods. Only four Grand Prix have been built to date, though Fraser may yet build more in his workshop at Marlborough, Wiltshire.*

Bottom left: *Racy Mini. Styled and built by ex-Lotus man Brian Luff, the Status Minipower was inspired by his disappointment with the Lotus Seven S4. Launched in 1971, the car was offered in kit form, its construction consisting of a tubular spaceframe chassis, double wishbone suspension at each corner and a simple glassfibre body. A Mini power unit slotted into the rear end, and though the car performed well and held the road like a racer, it went out of production in 1973 with only a small quantity built.*

225

The Nimrod's problem was that it did not appear until spring 1973–a time when the looming ugliness of VAT had just about exterminated the fun car boom. Hence only five of these front-engined, Mini-based machines were ever built, although the car could still be revived following the recent purchase of the moulds by an enthusiast.

Top left: *Another design from the prolific drawing board of stylist Barry Stimson, the Stimson Safari Six appeared late in 1971 and stayed in production until early 1973. Under the attractive glassfibre shell was a spaceframe chassis using complete Mini front end and four independently-sprung trailing arms for the rear wheels. About twenty examples were built.*

Bottom left: *Long established as a Hillman/Chrysler Imp-powered specialist car, the Davrian body/chassis unit was adapted for a Mini power unit in 1973. Nowadays the only motor car manufactured in Wales, the Davrian's rear-engined layout, lightweight all-glassfibre monocoque construction and superb roadholding have given it great success in both racing and rallying.*

227

City Mini. The very attractive Minissima was styled by Aston Martin Lagonda designer, William Towns, and displayed on the Austin/Morris stand at the 1973 Motor Show at Earls Court. Entry was through a single rear door, and

power was of course by Mini, with automatic transmission. Although British Leyland used the car as a publicity vehicle for two years, it was sadly never put into even limited production.

Truckin' Mini. One of Ranger Automotive's development projects in 1975 was this simple, four-wheeler pick-up version of the Ranger Cub. Things were kept simple with a set of standard Mini running gear, but only four of these vehicles were built before the company ran into trouble in 1976.

Opposite, top: *Called the Status 365, this practical 2 +2 machine was announced late in 1974, and over the next five years it was not unknown for owners to be asked if their car was perhaps the new generation Mini – despite its strange styling! In fact, the car was sold as a glassfibre and plywood monocoque body/chassis unit ready to accept a standard set of Mini subframes and running gear. Only a small number were built.*

Opposite, bottom: *If you had £265 in 1974, one way of spending it was on a Ranger Cub body/chassis unit. Then all you had to do was bolt into the front end a Mini subframe complete with engine, add Mini steering and a single trailing arm at the rear and you were almost ready to go. Based in Southend, Ranger Automotive claimed to have built no less than 200 Cubs before production ceased in 1976.*

230

Developed from the Stimson Mini Bug 2, the Stimson CS+II emerged in 1976 from a small workshop in Brighton. One year later the project was bought by a company called Mini Motors of Rochdale. Small numbers of body/chassis units had been supplied by the time the company was last heard of in 1979.

Opposite, top: *The Moke reborn? Well, no, quite, but in 1975 you could buy the next best thing, a Jimini. Using standard Mini subframes, the Jimini's all-steel body/chassis unit cost £300 in basic form. Only twelve examples of this type were built before the company suffered internal disputes which ended production for a few months.*

Opposite, bottom: *When it re-emerged in 1976 under a new company, the Jimini looked much more attractive with a sloping bonnet and square headlamps. Still in limited production, the car has reached production numbers of over 150 at the time of writing, including a couple of six-wheelers.*

232

233

Mini thingy. A three-seat three-wheeler ridden like a horse, steered like a car and powered by a Mini engine mounted open-fashion like a motorbike, it's difficult to say exactly what kind of vehicle the amazing Stimson Scorcher is!

234

Still, since its appearance in 1976 the Scorcher has given great pleasure and very economical motoring to about 30 enthusiasts, and does not go rusty either.

Having reached a production total of around 700, the first-generation Mini-Scamp was replaced by a Mk. 2 model in 1978. As ever, running gear was from the good old Mini, the main changes being in the bodywork department and with a stronger multi-tubular chassis. The Mini-Scamp Mk. 2 is still available at the time of writing, although the gullwing doors have been replaced by doors hinged in the normal fashion.

Opposite: Announced early in 1979, the Midas is surely the ultimate alternative Mini. It is superbly styled (by Richard Oakes), virtually 100% rustproof, highly economical, very practical thanks to its opening rear window and children's seats, capable of terrific roadholding and blessed with excellent performance. Built from an all-glassfibre monocoque structure, the Midas is sold by D & H Fibreglass Techniques of Greenfield, near Oldham.

236

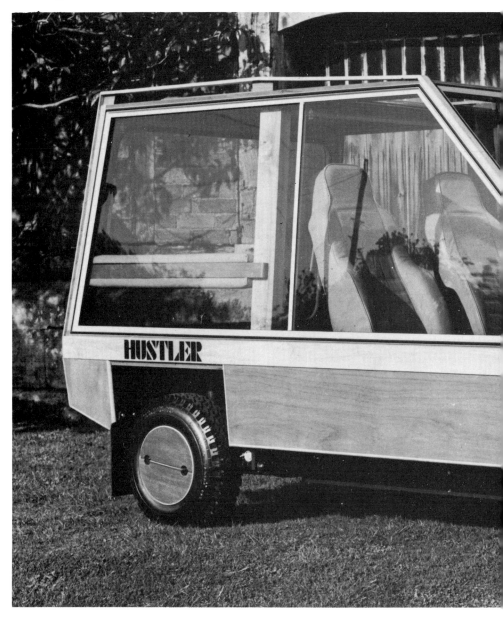

*One of William Towns' objectives with the Hustler project was versatility,
but he still managed to surprise everyone when he came up with his amazing
wooden Hustler in 1980–even more so when he offered, for around £600, a
set of detailed plans plus all components which were not wooden or could not*

be taken from the Mini. Actually, this is not as silly as it might sound, for the average carpenter can easily build the car's marine ply monocoque body/ chassis unit and perhaps get the whole show on the road for a total of around £1200.

Another recent Mini-based specialist car is the Magenta Sprint. Lightspeed Panels of Lealholm, near Whitby, have been building BMC 1100/1300-based Magentas for years, and in 1980 the company broadened its range with a Mini-

powered derivative. Only the front Mini subframe is used, the rear of the glass-fibre-bodied tubular chassis rides on Mini trailing arms and coil spring/damper units.

241

Following the construction in 1975 of what was only intended to be a one-off, the Nomad's designer, John Foers, decided to go ahead with a production version in 1977. Using straightforward Mini running gear, the Nomad was sold as a kit form, steel-panelled body/chassis unit. The company, Foers Engineering of Rotherham, found themselves gradually spending more and more time on the cars and less on its normal business making trailers and truck bodies. Convertible, pick-up and van versions of the Nomad are still available at the time of writing.

Trendy Mini. William Towns' concept for the Hustler was to provide the simplicity and all-round purpose of a Mini-Moke whilst introducing some of the civilisation of a car like the Range Rover. Available since 1979, the Hustler structure involves a substantial tubular steel spaceframe chassis, glassfibre lower body panels and two Mini subframes. Pick-up and six-wheeler versions of the car are also in existence.

8
More Mini

When this book was started some three years ago, it was simply a book about the versatility of the Mini, and had no great aspirations towards being a totally comprehensive study. But it soon became clear that the Mini demanded better treatment than a mere survey, because for every person who helped with each photograph or snippet of information there were almost always two or three more–friends, or friends of friends–who had something to add. Everyone, it seemed, had been involved with a Mini at sometime or other, and everyone remained enthusiastic enough to want to help. As if confirmation of the Mini's great following was ever needed, here was the sort of reaction that said it all!

So, what was originally one book soon became two; what was a straight-forward job soon turned into an exhaustive search for material covering every aspect of the Mini's impact worldwide. The idea of this chapter is to act as a brief sampler for the second book, at the same time adding further dimensions to the essential ingredients of the Mini story. No book on the Mini would be complete without photographs of a silly Mini, a mud-plugging Mini, a wild drag racing Mini, a home-built one-off using Mini parts, a hard working Mini, a Mini in some far away part of the world, or a racing Mini demolishing itself! The Mini was all these things and much more besides.

This chapter, then, is no more than a small taste of things to come. It has to be small because the Mini has achieved so much in its time that a sampler could not hope to give more than an inkling of what this amazing little character still has in store for us all. With the car still holding its own in showrooms, on racetracks, in coachbuilders' workshops and in private garages, there are sure to be several surprises yet. Indeed, perhaps the Mini story will never end . . .

Mud-plugging Mini. Apart from the more serious side of its competition career in racing and rallying, the Mini has had a lot of fun in a great variety of short circuit events. Photographed during a rallycross meeting at Kent's Lydden Hill circuit in 1970, this mucky Mini is just about to take a bath.

Opposite: *Sports racing Mini. During the 1960's Landar Components of Birmingham built about 40 examples of their pretty Landar R6 racers. Underneath the glassfibre body were a multi-tubular space frame chassis and a rear-mounted Mini engine. This is Frank Aston's car at Shelsey Walsh hillclimb.*

Working Mini. And a hard life it has had too, by the looks of things! Not one of the more picturesque sights of Moreton-in-Marsh, Gloucestershire; this mobile refreshment dispenser was nevertheless one of the established features of the town during the late 1970's.

Opposite: *Working Mini. Showing how marvellously adaptable the Mini has proved to be, this car has been converted to give maximum mobility to a disabled person otherwise restricted to a wheelchair.*

Mid-engined Mini. This remarkable one-off special was built during 1974 and 1975 by Birmingham man Derek Davenport. He used a multi-tubular space frame chassis and two Mini subframes, the rear one supporting a tuned 1300GT engine. The glassfibre bodywork was also entirely home built.

Gimmick Mini. All done to further the Mini image during the 1960's.

Matching Minis. The Minis few of us like to see. These particular ones are used by the Greater Manchester police.

Draggin' Mini. Using a moulded replica Mini bodyshell, Rob Messent and Roger Bishop's 'Stripteaser' was a well known drag racer during the 1970's When this shot was taken at Santa Pod, the car used Jaguar 3.8 litre power. Photograph: Mike Key.

Global Mini. Yes, Minis even found their way to the plains of Nevada, this one being pictured there in 1961.

Opposite: *Innocenti Mini. Styled by Bertone, this smart modern cousin of the standard Mini was introduced in 1974 and was built in Milan, Italy, from body panels and kits of running gear made by BL in Birmingham. Strangely enough, the car was never introduced on the home market.*

Incident Mini. This remarkable photograph was taken at Lydden Hill circuit in the late 1960's, appropriately enough during a 'novices' handicap race. The driver, Robert Mandry, was thankfully unhurt, and for his troubles, managed to appear on the front page of a national Sunday newspaper!

Opposite: *Metro Mini. Would any book on the Mini be complete without a picture of BL's new generation small car which still hasn't managed to replace Alec Issigonis' masterpiece?*